Euripides

IPHIGENIA AT AULIS
and
IPHIGENIA IN TAURIS

Translated and Introduced by

Robert Emmet Meagher

THOT

• CHATTANOOGA •

II

In Celebration of our Friendship

for

Michael Joyce

Any man who would prefer great wealth or power
to love, the love of friends,
is sick to the core of his soul.

• Euripides, *Herakles* •

_____

The good and decent man,
even if he lives in some distant place,
and even though I never set eyes on him,
I count as my friend.

• Euripidean fragment •

III

CONTENTS

IV

ACKNOWLEDGMENTS

I begin here in despair of doing my duty. The full listing of those deserving mention in this place would call for still another volume one step more esoteric than the present one. Painful as it is, I must be stoically select in print, and hope to make up for it later in person.

This volume is part of a project comprising a full-scale production of the Iphigenia plays, together with an extensive exploration of the history and culture of ancient Greece. The University of Tennessee at Chattanooga and the Girls Preparatory School are altogether central to this project. Their belief in and support of this endeavor in embryo made possible its birth. The Public Education Foundation and the Chattanooga Public Schools continue to play a gracious part in its development. Finally, without the American National Bank and the Lyndhurst Foundation, we would be making bricks without straw.

Behind impressive institutions, whether in Oz or in Chattanooga, however, stand even more impressive people. My debts are too many to settle here; but I will at least begin. My deep thanks to Cathy Barker, Donna Buckalew, Mary Carr, Marc Cutright, Aleta Davis, Maria Derrick, Robert Duffy, John Dyer, Kathy Frank, Bob Fulton, Paul Gaston, Cathie Ault Kasch, Margaret Kelley, Jim Lewis, Lu Lewis, Jan Mickler, Betsy Neave, Michael Quinn, Mary and Jeff Patchen, Sydney Roberts, Sharon Rose, Bo Sudderth, Jan Swafford, Randy Tucker, Grayson Walker and Terry Zimmer. It is a lasting privilege and joy to have shared this undertaking with them.

Beyond the immediate scope of this project, I wish to express my debt and appreciation to Michael Cacoyannis and Irene Papas. Without their friendship and inspiration, I would never have given my heart nor dug in my heels for this work which I so love. Finally, I wish to honor Michael Joyce as he has so often honored me with his kindness, humor and brilliance. The theatre is for him the most sacred of places, as is the world which it mirrors. Like altar boy to priest, I have knelt and wondered at him as much as at the mystery which we celebrate. It is all one.   R.E.M.

V

VI

INTRODUCTION

As I begin what is to be a brief introduction intended for the general reader, I confront a dilemma or, more honestly, a contradiction; for I am convinced that the plays of Euripides require no introduction. What they have to say, they can say, now as ever, for themselves. And they do, under certain conditions.

The conditions I have in mind are quite minimal. Ancient plays, preserved as texts in what is now a "dead" language, must first be translated and then staged if they are to live on. Once Euripides survives the translating table and is allowed to inhabit the theatre again, he speaks quite ably for himself. Regrettably, these conditions are seldom met, with the result that the voice of Euripides is rarely heard in our day. The loss is ours.

The heart of this volume, then, lies in the two texts which follow this introduction. These translations, like the originals which they imitate, are written for the theatre, to be staged first and studied next. A play printed on a page is like a butterfly pinned to a wall. We cannot say we have seen a butterfly until we have seen it on the wing; nor can we say we have seen Euripides until we have seen him on the stage. We are, then, in this introduction, far from the heart of the matter. With that acknowledged, I can go on. Criticism has been called the intellect's revenge on art. What I have in mind here is closer to reverence.

The Legend

It is not possible to place a date on the story of Iphigenia. Most stories worth telling over and over defy postmarks. Hers is no exception. The defining historical event at the center of her story -- the Trojan War -- may be placed, however, roughly where Herodotus put it long ago, in the thirteenth century before the common era. Although she may well have been sung in some lost Mycenaean epic, Iphigenia is never mentioned in Homer. Hesiod, on the other hand, is said to have told how Iphigenia, through the intervention of Artemis, managed to escape death forever and

VII

become herself the object of cult. A similar account is found in the post-Homeric epic, *The Kypria,* wherein Artemis, substituting a stag for the ill-fated girl, is said to have lifted her away to the land of the Taurians and transformed her into a goddess. Centuries later, in the fifth century, most notably in the theatre, Iphigenia made frequent appearances as sacrificial victim, sometimes rescued, sometimes not.

Regardless of its source, Iphigenia's story -- the story of her sacrifice at the hands of her own father and of her last-minute rescue at the hands of Artemis -- provides one of the most captivating stories in all of ancient literature, a story for our time as much as for any other. In its spell, cast all the more powerfully in the theatre, we come to see that the past is not past and that the darkest and brightest truths never change.

The Drama

What needs to be pointed out first is that the two plays in this volume were not written to be performed together. In the annual Dionysian theatrical festivals of Athens, each competing tragic playwright presented a set of four plays, comprised of a trilogy of often unrelated tragedies accompanied by a more brief and playful piece called a satyr drama. While placed side by side in this volume, the *Iphigenia at Aulis* and the *Iphigenia in Tauris* were written and first produced, in all likelihood, nearly ten years apart. The *Iphigenia at Aulis,* though first in this volume, was one of the last plays written by Euripides and was produced for him, together with the *Bakkhai* and the *Alkmaion,* posthumously, only months after his death. From his grave, Euripides won first prize with these last plays, something he had rarely accomplished while both he and his plays lived.

The arrangement of these two plays in this volume is, in the first place and most simply, for the sake of narrative integrity. Together, in two dramatic episodes, they tell the full drama of Iphigenia, providing for a modern audience the fullness of context required to appreciate either play on its own. Secondly, when we consider that the traditional ending of the *Iphigenia in Aulis,* beginning with lines 1532 in the

Greek text, is dismissed by most scholars as a contribution from some later anonymous donor, we may be justified in regarding the *Iphigenia in Tauris* in its entirety as the closest we can come to an authentically Euripidean conclusion to the unfortunately corrupted and compromised *Iphigenia at Aulis*. Judging from an Euripidean fragment, apparently from an *ex machina* promise by Artemis to send a doe as sacrificial substitute for Iphigenia, and knowing Euripides' penchant for wheeling out eleventh-hour divinities willing to suspend in the theatre fates that take their certain course everywhere else, it is perhaps safe to say that the original lost ending of the *Iphigenia at Aulis* called for the saving appearance of Artemis, doe in hand, much as Iphigenia herself described the event in the *Iphigenia in Tauris:* " . . . goddess Artemis stole me from the knife and fire, leaving a deer to bleed and burn in my stead, while I was blown through luminous aether here, to Taurica, a barbarous land with a barbarous king."

In moving from legend to drama, however, we must keep in mind the conventional license enjoyed by Greek playwrights to draw selectively from and to improvise freely upon traditional stories in sketching the plots of their plays. Although, with few exceptions, the tragic playwrights retold old stories, their retellings told as much about the present as about the past. In the hands of Euripides, the stories of the past were given precisely that light and slant and shape required for them to mirror the present with candor. For Euripides, a playwright in dark times, this meant disabusing his contemporaries of any illusions of stature and tragedy. In his dramas, Euripides gave a corrupt generation a suitably corrupted mythic structure in which to see itself as it was.

The Sacrifice

It is not possible to explore here every challenge hurled by Euripides at his own generation and, for that matter, at ours. There is one such challenge, however, from which his two Iphigenia plays permit no escape.

Central to both plays is the act of sacrifice, finally human sacrifice, an act unspeakable, an act on which our minds fall blank. Yet, if we fail to confront the idea and reality of sacrifice, in its many faces and forms, then we must fail to grasp these plays. And again the loss is ours. Euripides wrote, after all, not to entertain but to illumine. The ancient theatre was, as its name -- *theatron* -- suggests, a "seeing place," a place of insight, not distraction. The experience of these plays is thus to be an experience of heightened vision. Undoubtedly, the spectacle of human sacrifice, as well as the sight of a goddess miraculously interrupting the affair, would serve to dilate the eyes and imaginations of any witnesses. But Euripides has something more in mind than sheer spectacle and the voyeurism it provokes. If Euripides confronts his audience with the unthinkable, the unspeakable, it is to provoke thought and speech; not to suppress them. It has been said many times that the theatre of Euripides is a theatre of ideas. Perhaps that is why Socrates is said to have made a point of attending his plays. Regardless, if we inquire into the idea of sacrifice, we find ourselves at the heart of the plays at hand.

To anyone other than a practitioner the act of sacrifice is bound to seem barbaric. Surely its name is euphemistic. How, anyone might ask, does making someone dead also make them sacred? Sacrifice, it would seem, is a fancy word for slaughter. Anyone or any people who practice it have slipped back into savagery, crossed the line into bestiality. Or so it would seem to civilized common sense, as we know it today or as Euripides' fellow Athenians knew it then.

Common sense, however, is often neither. After all, it is humans, not beasts who practice sacrifice. Furthermore, many of the earliest traces and recollections of humanity's passage from nature to culture, from savagery to civilization, suggest that sacrifice served to distinguish human beings from the animals. Sacrifice, including human sacrifice, was and perhaps is a mark of the human, a foundation stone of civilization. Indeed, ample evidence of the practice of human sacrifice from the paleolithic period to the bronze age is depicted in the legend of Iphigenia, representing a continuity of tens of thousands of years. We, anyone who would eschew the practice of human sacrifice, may be the aberrant, inhuman ones. It is a possibility to be considered.

X

The act of ritual sacrifice was, quite simply, the central cultic act of ancient Greek religion, the sacred experience *par excellence.* In it the essential order of the universe was acknowledged and reinforced. The proper performance of sacrifice was seen as a stay against chaos rather than as a collapse into it.

The fundamental structure of the sacrificial act was twofold: ritual slaughter of the victim followed by a communal feasting on its flesh. Human victims were admittedly the exception. Human sacrifice and ritual cannibalism were reserved for moments of extreme peril or crisis. On Minoan Crete, for example, there is evidence of child sacrifice and homophagy to avert the imminent threat of earthquake. Another form of sacrifice, attested in legend, involved the ritual banishing or killing of *pharmakoi,* human or bestial "scapegoats," made to carry with them the burdensome evils of a community polluted by disease or crime, a ritual whose intended outcome was *katharsis,* purification. Another pretext for human sacrifice was the need for "weather magic" to avert famine or flooding or whatever. Finally, when armies met and found themselves on the brink of battle, the sacrifice of a virgin was sometimes indicated. Her blood, the first-blood of the ensuing conflict, whether as provocation or charm, somehow seemed a fitting prelude to murderous frenzy.

Before dismissing the act of sacrifice out of hand as an act born and bred in darkness, however, we must consider this: that the destruction of the victim is, in theory, for the sake of many others' survival. The slaughter is followed by a feast. The denial of life leads to a celebration of life. What begins as and appears to be boldly life-destroying becomes manifestly life-affirming. In surrendering or taking life, its sacred worth is re-discovered. Such is the theory of sacrifice.

It may be instructive to consider, as well, that there is nothing uniquely Greek about either the theory or the practice of human sacrifice. Abraham, the father of Jewish faith, was no less willing to slay his own child than was Agamemnon. The fact that he did not complete the act altered very little, except for Isaac. Later, when on the brink of battle Jephthah promised to Yahweh, in return for victory, a burnt offering, which turned out to be his own beloved daughter, his offering was accepted. No substitution was made. Neither, we know, was any substitution acceptable when Jesus prayed to his father for release. In the words of Caiphas, "It is better for one man to die for the people."

Death for the sake of life. One for the sake of the many. Herein lies the core conviction of ritual sacrifice. Such was the conviction of Paul and of the early Christian Church who saw Jesus as the perfect victim, the sacrificial lamb of God, slain for the many, his flesh and blood a feast for all of lost humanity. To the eyes of faith, the crucifix presents a glorious sight, while non-Christians stare at the same crucifix and see something altogether hideous, something unspeakable. A similar void opens up in the final scene of the *Bakkhai,* when the god abandons Agave to her own devices and to simple human sight. In that moment the brilliant trophy in her hand becomes the head of her own boy, fresh from his shoulders, ripped loose in what seemed at the time a joyous frenzy. Nowhere are the sacred and the profane so far apart as in the act and experience of sacrifice.

Whose vision, we must wonder, penetrates to the truth? When the god Dionysos releases Agave from his possession and her eyes see the hideous head in her hands, in that moment does she return to reality or does she depart from it? Which is the truth of the crucifix: atrocity or triumph? These questions bring us back to Iphigenia. Is she a martyr or a murder victim? A heroine or a "road-kill" on the way to Troy? And is there any difference?

Klytemnestra, the mother of Iphigenia, is clear on this much. Her daughter is being murdered by her own father. Everything else -- every appeal to a cause, a will or a compulsion higher and greater than a mother's love or a daughter's life -- is a pitiful screen thrown up between common decency and a vile crime. In the court of Klytemnestra, Agamemnon is without excuse. She is deaf to his invocations of Greece, necessity and the divine will. If there are gods, she says, we insult them when we murder in their name. In the *Iphigenia in Tauris,* Iphigenia has come around to her mother's assessment of sacrifice and of the goddess who supposedly craves and commands it. "Here in

XII

this land," she declares, "men, not gods, are murderers. Men make their own perversions into rituals and sacralize their sins. No god is evil. That is what I believe." It is also, I am convinced, what Euripides himself believed. This belief found simple and profound expression in the *Bakkhai* when the Chorus of women sang: "Those who scoff at the happiness of simple days and sweet nights, our god hates. It is ordinary wisdom to keep the mind away from extraordinary men and their excesses. Common sense and common decency. I aspire to nothing more." As for oracles claiming to speak for the gods and as for priests claiming to do the gods' will, in the *Helen* the Messenger, an ordinary, decent man, reiterates what I suspect to be the opinion of Euripides: "You know, now I see the art of prophecy for what it is, a vulgar occupation and a pack of lies . . . Best just to leave the priests alone . . . Anyway, the best magic is a balanced mind, and a little common sense."

What, then, are we to make of the appeals of Agamemnon to his daughter, for her to see his act -- his taking of her life -- in a different, higher light? His words to her are nothing less than a sermon, an outpouring not of reason but of faith. In this case, bad faith. Euripides leaves no room for doubt on this. By the time Agamemnon mounts his pulpit, it is too late for him to touch us with his words. We know too much. Iphigenia, on the other hand, knows too little.

After failing to convince his wife that he is in the grip of grander designs or, at the least, extenuating circumstances, Agamemnon turns to his daughter. He offers her a "higher" truth, an altered, heightened vision of what he is about to inflict and of what she is about to suffer. Beneath this aria, however, Euripides has also provided the base line, for all but Iphigenia to hear, the reality, as it were, beneath the hymn.

The Lie

The truth revealed early on in the *Iphigenia at Aulis* is that Agamemnon's ambition has outstripped both his abilities and his luck. He is no more in control of his army than he is of the weather. The army has reasons of its own for sailing to Troy, and they have nothing to do with retrieving Helen or restoring Greek pride. The army is hellbent on violence and plunder. Meanwhile, Agamemnon is so enamored of his prerogatives and so enslaved by his fears, that he is willing to murder his own beloved girl rather than compromise his career or confront the truth. And not only does he dispatch his daughter to death, but he sends her off embracing a seductive lie, whose perversity she is both too callow and too desperate to detect. In other words, he takes advantage not only of her weakness but also of her innocence.

There is no reason for imagining that Agamemnon believes a word of what he tells Iphigenia regarding why she must die. In utterly lucid bad faith, Agamemnon creates a lie the size of the atrocity he is willing and about to commit. He invents Hellas, Greece, an entity greater than the sum of all of its living daughters and sons; and so it must be if it is to demand and to justify their deaths, as many as may be needed. He invents too the barbarians as a people whose very existence is an affront and a threat, and whose extinction or subjection constitutes a moral imperative. In short, Agamemnon invents, before our eyes, politics.

What so darkens and complicates this tragedy is that Iphigenia is being murdered by her own father, a truth which neither Agamemnon nor Iphigenia is able to look straight in the face. Instead, they agree to share a consoling lie. He plants it, and she carries it to term. Greece, he says, is turning to him and to her and demanding of them the ultimate sacrifice. Nothing less than the freedom of Greece is at stake. With this lie, Agamemnon anaesthetizes his girl before putting her under the knife. Never should we mistake this act, however, for one of compassion. Anaesthesia, after all, is administered as much for the surgeon's convenience as for the patient's comfort. In this instance, Agamemnon's prevailing concern is to ease his own passage to Troy, not his daughter's passage to Hades. Her death is something he wants to put behind him with as little awkwardness and delay as possible.

The *Iphigenia at Aulis* is Euripides' last word on war, the politics which provoke it, and the victims who endure it.

No war would ever be fought without seducing the young to its awful momentum. Young, beautiful bodies and souls must be given some compelling reason for dying or killing; and those whose purposes are served by war know that the truth will not do. It is cursedly the case that the inexperience, idealism, passion and naiveté of youth conspire to make them prey to the speeches of their elders. The timeless scandal is that the latter, like Agamemnon, know both the power of their words and their emptiness.

The Conversion

For many critics, ancient and modern, the radical conversion of Iphigenia to her fate is too sudden and too complete to be believed or accepted. One moment, Iphigenia begs on her knees for her life. She longs for the persuasive powers of Orpheus and uses her younger brother instead to try to break down her father's murderous resolve. Running out of words, she reminds her father that "to look upon the light of day is for all of us the sweetest of joys. In the dark world below there is nothing. To pray for death is sheer madness. To be alive, in whatever lowly condition, is better than to die a glorious death." It is not long, however, before Iphigenia, resolving not to clutch her life too tightly or, for that matter, at all, offers herself freely to just such a "glorious" death. "I give my life to Greece," she announces. "Sacrifice me and lay waste to Troy." Her last speech has clearly been scripted by her father. She has swallowed his words as if they were the sweetest milk.

There is much that could be said to anyone, including Aristotle, disappointed by Iphigenia's change of heart; but it all comes down to this. She knows she is lost. Worse, she knows her own father is going to kill her. She has only one last choice to make and only moments in which to make it: whether to die a hideous death at the hands of a father turned maniac or to die a martyr to a cause so bright as to cast out forever the darkness of this moment. Of course, this choice exists in her mind and nowhere else. Its only effect is that, for her few remaining breaths, she may be able not to hate her own father, to believe in his love and to imagine that he

XV

knows more than she does. Who, I wonder, can begrudge her this? Besides, it is all sadly true.

The Miracle

As for the miraculous and salvific appearance of Artemis and all that follows upon it, we do well to enjoy it while we can. It was meant for our delight, the delight available in the theatre where life is only watched and not lived and where any of life's necessities may be reversed or altered at will. Euripides wrote a number of plays whose darkness is lifted in the last instant by a visitor from on high, a divine aunt or uncle, as it were, carrying the one gift we most desire. He went even further, in fact, and wrote what are best described as romantic melodramas or comedies, plays seasoned throughout with levity and humor and ending with a promise of happiness forever after. Such are the lost endings of the *Iphigenia at Aulis* and the entirety of the *Iphigenia in Tauris,* ironic escapes from what admits of no escape, playful exceptions which serve only to prove the rule. In realizing how close laughter is to tears and in exploring their border, Euripides extended the meaning of *katharsis,* the purifying release from inner pain and pollution which was to be the climax of the tragic experience.

The Translation

The two translations in this volume are intended for performance, not primarily for academic study. Most translations of ancient plays are written for the desk or for the lap, to be examined as cultural fossils or to be read as poetry. Very few translations of Greek tragedy are written for the stage. Actors and directors, in reading through a script, know at once whether it is actable, whether it will play. The lyrics of the chorus must be able to be set to music and danced. The dialogue must ring true. The characters must be convincing as they reveal themselves in their words. Insults must be insulting. Rage must be resonant in the language used to convey it. Humor must be funny on the face of it. If we are required to learn from program notes that what one

XVI

character just said to another would have been an insult or would have been a joke in the theatre of Dionysos, then we are not watching a play. We are reading about one. A book allows for cross-referencing and for back-scanning. If we don't get something, we can look it up or read it again. Not so in a play, which, like music, either carries us with it or leaves us behind. In short, the first commandment to be observed in translating a play is that thou shalt not make a good play into a bad play, much less into a poem or a study guide. This, to my mind, is the appropriate meaning of "literal" translation. It is also the goal I set for myself in the translations which follow.

XVIII

IPHIGENIA AT AULIS

CHARACTERS
In Order of Appearance

Agamemnon
High King of the Greek Forces

Old Servant
Slave in the House of Agamemnon

Chorus
Young Women from Khalkis
        and Attendants to Klytemnestra and Iphigenia

Choral Leader
Leader of the Chorus

Menelaos
Brother of Agamemnon and Husband of Helen

Klytemnestra
Wife of Agamemnon

Iphigenia
Daughter of Agamemnon and Klytemnestra

Messenger
In the Entourage of Klytemnestra

Orestes
Brother of Iphigenia,
        Son of Agamemnon and Klytemnestra

Akhilleus
Greatest of the Greek Warriors

2

The scene is Agamemnon's camp at Aulis.   It is night. Agamemnon enters from his tent and looks around in the darkness for his Old Servant, who is lying awake and unseen off to one side.

Agamemnon

Calling out to his Old Servant.

Old one, come here. . . to the front of my tent.

Old Servant

From offstage.

I'm coming.
What is it, lord Agamemnon?

Agamemnon

I want you to hurry!

Old Servant

Entering.

I *am* hurrying! I'm certainly not sleeping.
At my age, I lie down . . . that's it.

Agamemnon

Tell me. What star is that directly over us?

Old Servant

Near the Pleiades . . . it's Sirius,
          square in the middle of the sky.

Agamemnon

Listen. Nothing.
Not a sound.
Not from a single bird.
Even the sea is still.
The river too is mute . . . without the winds.

3

Old Servant

My lord, what are you doing out here
        in the middle of the night?
There's nothing but peace and quiet in Aulis.
Not even our own sentries are stirring.
Why don't we go inside?

*Agamemnon nods and turns to re-enter his tent, gesturing to
the Old Servant to follow him inside.*

Agamemnon

O how I envy you, old one.
I envy anyone who can live a life without risk,
        unnoticed, free of fame.
In fact, the more significant a man is,
        the more I pity him.

Old Servant

Just what do you pity in a man who has everything?

Agamemnon

The fact that everything he has can, and probably will,
        slip away.
Privilege is sweet one day and bitter the next.
When the gods slip, it's we who fall.
And when we land on our feet,
        our fellow mortals wait for us,
                sleeplessly scheming our ruin.

Old Servant

I have trouble hearing such laments
        coming from a king.
Lord Agamemnon, Atreus fathered you into the world,
        not paradise.
Down here, in addition to enjoying yourself,
        you must suffer.
Even you were born mortal.

So, with or without your consent, the will of the gods
     is what's going to happen.
But tell me . . .
Your lamp burning bright at this hour . . .
     and these tablets . . .
I can see you've been writing something . . .
     and that you still hold it in your hand,
          sealed and broken open many times . . .
              written and unwritten,
          hurled to the ground and written again.
I heard you weeping.
Now I see that you soaked the ground with your tears.
Whatever it is you're struggling with,
     you seem to be losing . . .
          at least your wits.

*Agamemnon slumps into a chair, lowering his head into
his hands and weeping.*

What is it, my king? What new shadow pursues you?
Tell me everything. Let me into your pain.
You don't need walls against a simple, decent man,
     someone you know you can trust.
Remember, I've been with you a long time,
     from the day Tyndareos sent me
     with your bride, a worthy item in her dowry.

Agamemnon

Phoibe, my wife Klytemnestra, and Helen.
Those were the three sisters born to Leda,
     daughter of Thestios.
Now when Helen's time arrived, her suitors came
     from every corner of Greece, young men who
          already had everything . . . except Helen.
They whiled away their time together boasting
     and making dark threats, in case they failed,
          promising to slay the one among them
              whose dream would have come true.
All the while Tyndareos was torn two ways.

5

He could either go on with the marriage or call it off;
        and it was difficult to predict
                which would be the more disastrous.
Then it came to him.
He would unite all the suitors in a common oath,
        sealed with a burnt offering to make it last.
And so the famous pact came to be.
The suitors one and all swore to stand behind, not against,
        the fortunate groom, whoever it might be.
If anyone, barbarian or Greek,
        should ever drive Helen's husband from his bed
                and carry her away,
        together they would march against that fool's city
                and raze it to the ground.
So, duped by an old and clever man,
        the suitors made their oath.
And to his daughter Tyndareos gave the final word.
Hers would be a love-choice.
Helen would lift her heart's sail,
        and watch the winds of desire do the rest.
Somehow that meant Menelaos.
Looking back, I wish it had been anyone else.
Then, fresh from his famous beauty contest,
        a Phrygian dandy made his way to Sparta.
It was Paris, in the bloom of youthful beauty and allure,
        swathed in silks, appointed in gold,
                Paris at his barbarian best.
There was love at once between them . . . Helen and Paris.
As soon as Menelaos went away, the herdsman from Troy
        snatched up his prize and brought her back
                to graze on the slopes of Ida.
Next came the fury of her lawful spouse,
        who made the rounds of Helen's one-time suitors,
                unearthing an old promise,
        invoking a consortium of revenge.

As it happened, all of Greece ran for its arms,
        launched itself and got just this far,
                to the straits of Aulis,
                        where every sail went limp.

6

Ships, armor, horses, chariots . . .
        all beached now on the strand.
And I am in command, by acclamation.
I suppose because I am the brother of the cuckold.
It is an honor I would be relieved to wish on anyone else.
So, here we are, an army in full muster,
        a fleet trimmed to sail.
All we lack is wind.

And for that, Khalkis the seer found the solution.
To Artemis, who prevails in this place,
        I am to sacrifice my own daughter Iphigenia.
If I do this, our sails will fill with wind,
        and Troy will fall.
Neither will happen if I don't.

When I first heard this "solution,"
        I told Talthybios our herald
            to proclaim in his loudest voice
        that the army was dismissed.
Never would I be willing to kill my own child.
It was my own brother who laid siege to me then
        with every argument he could conjure,
            until he had my hands willing to do
        what my heart could not even imagine.
I inscribed a tablet and dispatched it to my wife,
        telling her to send our daughter here to Aulis
            to be wed to Akhilleus.
I shared with her my excitement
        over the stature of this man
            our daughter would marry,
        adding that Akhilleus was refusing to sail to Troy
        unless his house and ours were bound in marriage.

All this -- the whole story of our daughter's marriage --
        I made up, a ruse
            to get my wife to play into our hands.
Kalkhas, Odysseus, Menelaos: they were there with me.

No one else knew anything.

7

Then I came to my senses.
In the benign obscurity of night, on a fresh tablet,
        I untold my own lie, sealing it, unsealing it . . .
But that you already know.

Picking up a tablet and handing it to the Old Servant.

Old one, go.
Take this tablet to Argos.
It holds a deep secret.
And, knowing your loyalty, I will tell you what it is.
This is what I have written:
"Daughter of Leda, contrary to what I wrote earlier . . . "

Agamemnon pauses and does not go on.

Old Servant

Go on. Tell me the heart of the message,
        so that, if need be, I can deliver it verbally,
                exactly as you've written it.

Agamemnon

"Do not send your daughter to the calm shores of Aulis,
        braced by Euboea against the sea's wild moods.
We will celebrate the marriage of our girl
        another place, another time."

Old Servant

What about Akhilleus?
Suddenly single again, won't he explode . . .
        in the direction of you and your wife?
The wrath of Akhilleus is a dreadful thing.
Give me some idea what you will say
        when confronted with it.

Agamemnon

His wedding was not fact but a fiction,
        in which he was our unwitting accomplice.

Akhilleus knew nothing of the proposed marriage,
        much less of our real plans.
So far as he knows,
        I've never promised my daughter to his bed.

Old Servant

I see.
A blood victim for your army and a bride for Akhilleus.
A war and a wedding . . .
        your own daughter would provide both.
All you had to do was lie a little.
Lord Agamemnon, the flames you were lighting . . .
        did you think you would be able to put them out?

Agamemnon

I didn't think at all.
I leapt into the flames instead, in the hope of going mad.
But now, go . . . go, old one. Don't listen to your feet.
Stop for nothing.

Old Servant

I'm not going to waste any time.

Agamemnon

Then, when you reach the shade of the forest
        and the cool springs, don't stop.
Fight off sleep.

Old Servant

God forbid!

Agamemnon

Whatever you do, when you reach the fork in the road,
        keep your eyes open
                and watch for a chariot carrying Iphigenia
        along the shore road toward the ships.
It may be moving very fast; so don't let it slip by you.

9

Old Servant

As you say my, lord.

Agamemnon

Assuming she is already on her way,
        when you come upon her and her escorts,
            block their way.
Grab the bridles of their horses, giving them no choice
        but to turn around and go back
            to the walls the Cyclops built.

Old Servant

So I tell your wife and daughter to turn around
        and go back where they came from.
But why should they listen to me?

Agamemnon

Here.
Take this ring.
It bears my seal.
The same seal is on the tablet you carry.

Now go.
Already the four-horsed flames of Helios and his chariot
        advance upon the night.
It will be light soon.
Go.
Do your best for me.

The Old Servant exits.

Agamemnon

For us mortals, life is a brief moment.
Even so it is outlasts our longest joys.
Pain waits somewhere for each of us.

Agamemnon returns to his tent.
The Chorus enters.

10

Chorus

From nearby Khalkis my homeland, where
With the sea on every side
The famed waters of Arethusa
Find their radiant source,
We have crossed the swirling straits of Euripos,
Steering a course to Aulis,
Beaching our boat on these sandy shores.
We come here for one thing:
To see with our own eyes
The Akhaean host, the fleet sailed by men
Who might as well be gods.
We came to see the thousand ships.
Sent -- our own men say --
By fair-haired Menelaos
And high-born Agamemnon
To bring back Helen.
Paris, the herdsman-prince
Collected her from the reed-lined banks of the Eurotas
As a token from Aphrodite,
For that day when she stepped from her bath
To do battle with Hera
And Pallas Athena,
Drawing her beauty
Like a glistening sword.

Too excited to walk,
We ran just now
Through the grove of Artemis,
Over ground soaked with sacrifice,
To reach the camp.
We blush to admit
How much we wanted to see
Their tents, hung with war-gear,
Their burnished shields stacked into a wall around them,
Men on the verge of war,
Armed and mounted,
The swelling might of Greece.

First I caught sight of the two Aiases,
One the son of Oileos,
The other the son of Telamon
And held to be the crowning pride of Salamis.
With these two was Palamedes,
Whose grandfather is Poseidon himself.
The three of them sat bent over a game board,
Addicted to its demands,
Each one enthralled with his own cleverness.
Meanwhile, Diomedes threw the discus,
With visible solitary pleasure.
Nearby stood Meriones, an astonishing sight.
The blood of Ares runs in his veins.
I saw too the son of Laertes, from craggy Ithaka;
And then Nireus who, in beauty, stands all alone.

Next my eyes fell on the child of Thetis,
Tutored into perfection by the centaur Kheiron,
Akhilleus, whose feet, as if wings,
Carry him aloft.
Like a sudden burst of wind,
He ran the expanse of the beach.
It was a race:
Akhilleus in full armor and bare feet
Against a four-horsed war-chariot
Driven by a son of the house of Pheres,
Eumelos,
Who was trying to shout and goad his team
Out of their imminent defeat.
What a lovely sight they were:
Four perfect foals bridled in gold,
The middle two -- the yoke pair -- dappled gray
With flecks of white in their manes;
And the other two -- the trace pair -- bays
With spotted fetlocks.
I gazed at them as they drove hard and close
Around the turning-post,
With the son of Peleus so near
That his armor clanged against the chariot's railing
And made the wheels sing.

12

Not even the gods have words for what I saw next:
The spectacle of the ships.
My woman's eyes drank in that sight
With the pleasure I can still taste.
On the far right lay the fleet of the Myrmidons from Phthia,
Fifty sleek, sea-skimming vessels,
Their up-curved sterns crowned with the figures of Nereids,
Divine daughters of the sea, wrought in gleaming gold,
Emblems of Nereid-born Akhilleus.

Next and comparable to these were the Argive ships
Under the command of Mekistes,
The son and product of Talaos.
Beside him Sthenelos, Kampaneos' child.
Further to the left lay the Attic fleet,
Fifty ships bearing the image of goddess Athena
Mounted in a sky-borne chariot
Drawn by a team of winged horses,
A bright omen for the sailors who man those decks
And for the son of Theseus who leads them.

My gaze then fell on the Boetian contingent,
Fifty more emblazoned ships fitted out for war.
This time it was Kadmos and a golden dragon
Perched on the ships' sterns;
And it was Leitos the earth-born who led them.
There too was the son of Oileos, who sailed
To Aulis from the famed city of Thronion in Phokis,
With a fleet of fifty Lokrian vessels.

Next from Mykene whose walls the Kyklops set in place,
The son of Atreus filled a hundred ships with men
And brought them here.
He and his brother, sharing the high-command,
Share a common purpose too.
In the name of all Greece,
They will make Helen pay for what she did,
Turning her back on where she belonged
In heat for some barbarian's bed.

Then, from its blazonry,
I recognized the fleet of Geranian Nestor . . .
Atop each ship the Pylian River Alpheos,
In the image of a bull.

I counted twelve Ainian vessels next,
Under the command of their king Gouneos.
And, immediately beside these, the ships of Elis,
Commanded by Eurytos.
Right there at hand I saw the lords of Elis,
Whom everyone calls the Epeians.

Next there were the white-oared Taphian galleys
Under Meges, son of Phyleos.
These had sailed from the islands of Echinai
Whose rocky shores other sailors shudder to approach.

Now, on the extreme left flank of the armada,
My eyes fell on Aias of Salamis,
With the twelve most trim, agile craft of all,
Charged with keeping the entire fleet
Drawn up in order,
Moving as one,
Like a great net sweeping the seas.

This is what I have seen . . .
A vast host under sail.
God help any barbarians in boats
Who cross its path.
They will never see their homes again.

Later, years from now,
When the stories come back
And fill the halls of my house,
I will listen to them and remember
That here, today,
With my own eyes,
I saw it all begin.

The Chorus exits.

14

Menelaos and the Old Servant enter, engaged in a bitter quarrel. Menelaos carries in his hand the tablet.

Old Servant
Menelaos, you can't do this. You're going too far!

Menelaos
Get lost, old man! You're the one who went too far.
You're too loyal to your master.

Old Servant
Thank you. I take that as a compliment.

Menelaos
You're going to regret not learning your place.

Old Servant
And is it your place to read a message I was carrying
    for someone else?

Menelaos
What you were carrying was mischief . . . for all of us.
You haven't that right.

Old Servant
Argue that point somewhere else.
Just give me back the tablet.

15

Menelaos

No way.

Old Servant

Seizing the tablet

Then neither will I.

Menelaos

All right.

Brandishing his sceptre.

In that case I'll club your head to a bloody pulp.

Old Servant

It would be an honor to die for my master.

Menelaos

Raising his sceptre to strike the Old Servant

You have a big mouth for a slave.

Re-enter Agamemnon. The Old Servant drops at once to one knee and reaches out his hands toward Agamemnon. As he does so, Menelaos snatches back the tablet.

Old Servant

My king, we have been wronged.
This man tore your tablet from my hands.
He doesn't care about right and wrong.

Agamemnon

Enough of this racket!
So. You choose the front of my tent to hold your quarrel.
Why?

Agamemnon turns his back on them both.

Menelaos

I think it is my place to speak first . . . before him.

Agamemnon

Then explain your private war with him . . .
     and your use of force.

Menelaos

Turn around and look me in the eye.
Then I'll say what I have to say.

*Agamemnon turns around to face Menelaos.   As the
argument between them heats up and catches fire, the Old
Servant exits.*

Agamemnon

Son of Atreus, if I prefer not to look at you,
     do you really think it's out of fear ?

Menelaos

Then look at this tablet and the foul treason it contains.

Agamemnon

I'm looking.
Now give it back to me.

Menelaos

Opening the tablet.

No, not until I read it . . .
     loud enough for every Greek to hear.

Agamemnon

So, you've broken my seal . . .
     and learned what is none of your business.

Menelaos

Learned all about your treachery, you mean.
It's something you will pay for.

Agamemnon

How was it you intercepted him?
God, you have your nerve!

Menelaos

I was actually looking for your daughter,
         to see if she had arrived yet from Argos.

Agamemnon

You really are shameless.
What persuaded you to pry into my affairs?

Menelaos

I persuaded myself.
I was born your brother, not your slave.

Agamemnon

So what?
Is someone else going to keep my house?
I don't like the sound of that.

Menelaos

I'll tell you what I don't like. Forget your house.
You can't keep your own head straight.
A few days ago you felt one way;
         now you feel another way.
I'm sure if we wait around a while longer . . .

Agamemnon

You certainly have a way with vicious words.
Your kind of eloquence is a disease, you know.

Menelaos

And what about a mind that changes like the weather,
        or a heart that betrays today yesterday's friends?
Signs of health?

Now it is my turn, Agamemnon, to indict you.
Try not to let your anger blind you
        to the truth in what I say.
And I, for my part, will try not to go too far.

Surely you remember how keen you were at first to lead
        the Greeks to Troy, although you did your best
            not to let it show.
You put on your humblest airs,
        and you shook nearly every hand in Greece.
At your palace it was all "open doors" and "first names."
You made constant conversation,
        whether anyone wanted it or not.
With mere tokens, you tried to buy your way into power.
And it worked.

So, sceptre in hand, you quickly changed your ways.
You dropped your friends like leaves off a tree.
You lived behind bolted doors.
You had time for no one.
When a decent man succeeds and rises in the world,
        he holds his ground, an anchor of trust,
            especially for his friends.
His good fortune becomes theirs.
Somehow the opposite was true with you.
I have mentioned this first,
because it was my first quarrel with you.

King of kings, commander-in-chief of the Greek forces . . .
        that was you when you first came to Aulis.
Soon you were a non-entity.
Limp sails -- one token of divine displeasure --
        and you fell apart.
Your army had enough of futility and shouted to go home.
Meanwhile, your wretchedness was etched across your face.

19

The vision of a thousand ships and of a vast host of men
        thronging the plains of Troy,
                all under your command . . .
        the vision was fading and you were desperate.
You called for me.
"What do I do? What way is there out of this?"
"I can't just give up my command,
        let fame run out between my fingers like water.
There must be something I can do. What is it?"
This was your question to me . . .
        to which Kalkhas found the answer . . .
                somewhere in the bowels of his birds.
He told you to sacrifice your daughter to Artemis.
Then your ships would sail.
You breathed easy and seemed almost light-hearted as
        you promised to bring your daughter to the blade.
When you sent for her, telling your wife
        to bundle off the girl at once,
                as would-be bride for Akhilleus,
        you did so on your own . . . don't deny it.
No one twisted your arm. No one had to.

Then you changed your mind and sent a second message,
        revoking the first.
Now you say, "Never will I murder my own child."
Indeed. I call upon the sky above, where the gods dwell,
        to witness what you've said.
In fact, you couldn't be more trite.
The arduous climb to power only to plummet to ruin . . .
        it's an old story . . . with a couple of variations:
Sometimes it is the fault of the followers.
They forget how to follow.
Sometimes it is the fault of the leaders.
They forget how to lead . . . or, as in your case,
        they discover that they never knew how.
Still, I save my pity for Greece, hapless Greece,
        poised for the bold and brilliant stroke,
                yet doomed to be a joke for barbarians,
        laughing from their walls at the army that never came.
All because of your daughter.

20

No one should sit on a throne or lead an army because he
       shook a few hands or collected a few old debts.
Kings and generals need minds that work,
       producing an idea every now and then.

Choral Leader

It is a dark, disturbing sight,
       when brothers are locked in hate,
          and savage each other with their words.

Agamemnon

It is my turn now.
Unlike you, I will be brief, careful, and moderate.
You can see already the difference in my eyes.
I speak to you as a brother,
       and as one who knows the meaning of shame.
There's blood in your eyes and hate on your tongue.
Can you tell me why? Who has wronged you?
What is it that you want . . . a faithful wife?
Is that what your whining is about?
If so, I can't help you. Remember, you had a wife once.
You just did a bad job of keeping her.
And who should pay the price for that? *Me?*
For what went on, or didn't, in *your* bed?
Or is it the honors I've received: my stature, my power . . .
       have they gotten under your skin?
No. You're worked up over a woman.
I can tell from the way you've stopped thinking,
       and lost all sense of shame.
You just want a woman, don't you?
For a man like you, with no pride,
       desire can be a pretty shabby thing.

Now back to me.
If I, having made a mistake,
       recognize my error and correct it,
          does that make me a madman?
No, you're the one who's mad.
The gods did you a favor, ridding you of a worthless wife;
       and all you can think about is getting her back.

21

Long ago, Helen's love-sick suitors took Tyndareos' oath
        for all the wrong reasons.
Something or someone drove them to it,
        and it surely wasn't you.
Let's say a god called Hope did it.
So go ahead, take them on a war.
They're game for any lunacy you have in mind.
But don't assume the same of god.
The air up there is clearer than down here.
Mindless oaths taken in heat are seen as such.
I'm not going to kill any child of mine.
Besides, what kind of luck or blessing do you expect
        on this misadventure of yours?
You get perverse revenge on the worst wife that ever was,
        and I spend the rest of my days and nights in tears,
        wasting away, as I should, for what I did,
                against all law and sense,
                        against my own flesh and blood.
That is all I have to say,
        words as brief and wise and congenial
                as I could make them.
You can prefer madness if you like;
        but I'm going to keep my house in order.

Choral Leader

Agamemnon, this is not what you said before,
        but it is welcome;
                for it means life, not death, for your child.

Menelaos

I see I have no one left on my side.

Agamemnon

Why should you,
        when you're willing to kill those closest to you?

Menelaos

How can you call yourself my brother?

Agamemnon

You leave your senses and I leave you . . . why not?
Get your mind back and you get me back.

Menelaos

What about friends . . . don't they share each other's pain?

Agamemnon

I'll gladly share your pain . . . when you stop causing mine.

Menelaos

Forget me. Think of Greece!
Should you stand off from her struggles?

Agamemnon

Yes. It's all the same.
You and Greece share the same disease.
Whatever you've got is bigger than both of you.

Menelaos

Big words . . . from the man with the sceptre.
To your own brother you're a traitor.
Fortunately I have other friends and other ways of . . .

The Messenger enters.

Messenger

Agamemnon, High King of the Greeks,
         I come to you bringing your daughter, Iphigenia.
She is accompanied by her mother, your wife, Klytemnestra.
And, as a special treat for your eyes,
         your little boy, Orestes, too is here.
Already it has been too long since you saw him last.
They've endured a long, tiring journey.
They are refreshing themselves now, dipping their feet
         in the coolness of a nearby spring. Meanwhile,
         we've put their horses out into the meadow to graze.

23

I've run ahead to give you word of their arrival,
          so that you might be prepared for them.
The men already know your daughter's here.
Word travels fast through the ranks.
The whole army lined up along the road,
          just to get a look at her.
That's about as close as ordinary people get
          to magnificence . . . staring at it for a moment.
Anyway, the army is asking questions.
They want to know what's happening. A marriage, or what?
They wonder whether you missed your daughter so much
          that you had her brought to you.
I also heard them saying that it was all well and good to bring
          the child to the altar of Artemis, Mistress of Aulis,
                    in preparation for her wedding.
But who's the bridegroom?
That's what they really want to know.
So . . . where's the basket of barley for the sacrifice?
Come on, both of you . . . yes, you too, lord Menelaos,
          it's time to crown your heads with garlands.
The moment is coming for the wedding song.
Let the flute's piercing cry leap into the air
          and call everyone from the tents.
Let's dance and beat the earth with our feet like a giant drum.
For this is the day your daughter learns the meaning of bliss.

Agamemnon

Yes . . . thank you. You may go now.
As for the rest, it will go as well as it can in the hands of fate.

The Messenger exits.

Agamemnon

What a wreck of a man I am.
How do I begin over from here?
I'm so tangled in my own fate I can't move.
I counted on my cleverness . . .
          on staying two steps ahead of doom.
One leap took care of that.

24

I see now that the common people have their privileges.
They can share their pain
        and cry their hearts out, if they need to.
Not like us. We sit apart on our thrones,
        slaves to the people we purportedly rule.
I'm ashamed to cry . . . so alone, so ruined.
Yet, I hurt so much I'd be ashamed not to cry.
What do I say to my wife?
What kind of greeting do I give,
        when I can't even look her in the eyes?
On top of everything else, for her to come here now,
        in the middle of this . . . I can't . . .
I sent for my daughter not my wife!
Well . . . it's understandable . . .
        a mother wanting to accompany her daughter,
                wanting to be there
        to give her precious girl away.
But it means she will find out what I've done.
And the unlucky bride? Bride indeed.
Hades will see to that.
She will consummate her marriage in hell.
O my god. I can already hear what she will say to me.
"Father, are you really going to kill me? If so
        I hope that you and whoever is dear to you
        someday know a wedding night as long and cold
        as mine shall be."
Orestes too will barely stand nearby, sobbing.
In time he will understand why.
Priam's son has created a masterpiece of chaos
        from what used to be my life, a life that ended
                the day Helen climbed into his bed.

Choral Leader

I am a woman from a land far from yours;
        yet I feel close to your pain.
A sorry king is a pitiable sight.

Menelaos

Brother, give me your hand. I want to hold you.

25

Agamemnon

Here. You win. I lose.

Menelaos

Agamemnon, I swear by Pelops our grandfather
        and Atreus our own father, that I speak to you now
                straight from my heart.
What I say is what I truly think and feel,
        nothing more, nothing less.
The sight of you in tears
        has pried open my soul to your pain.
Like you, I have had a change of heart
        and now take back my own words.
You have nothing any longer to fear from me.
We are at one.
Don't take your child's life.
Not for my sake.
There is nothing fair about your grieving on and on,
        so that I might know a moment's satisfaction.
Nor is it right for your child to go dark in death,
        while mine revels in the light.

And what about me?
If I develop a craving to be married again,
        I can always take another bride.
But the last thing I can afford
        is to lose my brother.
I can think of no worse trade than you for Helen . . .
        treasure for trash.
I've been a child lately, without sense,
        watching this whole affair from too safe a distance.
Now that I'm closer, I see what it means
        for you to murder your daughter.
Besides, when I remember that the poor piteous girl,
        soon to be a victim to my marriage,
            is my family, too,
        my own feelings for her well up within me.
"Why Iphigenia?" I ask myself.
"What does she have to do with Helen?"

26

So I say, disband the army and send it home from Aulis.
For my sake if not for yours, brother,
        stop crying . . . so that I can.
Whether the words of Artemis regarding your daughter
        still speak to you or not,
        they say nothing to me.
I leave the matter with you.

In short, I've changed my mind.
No more bitter words, not from me.
The fact is I've stumbled onto where I belong . . .
        with you, dear brother.
It's been a struggle to find my way here.
I guess I can't be all bad if I kept trying.

Choral Leader

Menelaos, you have spoken like a true son of Tantalos,
        child of Zeus.
Your ancestors would be proud of you.

Agamemnon

Menelaos, I honor you and your words.
What you have said,
        with such becoming candor and integrity,
                has put the two of us in perfect accord.
We both know how easy and common it is for brothers,
        confused by lust or greed,
                to quarrel over a woman or an estate.
Enmity between brothers is a poison.
I spit it out once and for all.
But the truth is that our shoulders are against a fate
        that will not give way.
I have no choice anymore.
I am compelled to kill my daughter.

Menelaos

Compelled?
By whom?

Agamemnon

By the army we gathered.

Menelaos

No. Not if you send your daughter back to Argos first.

Agamemnon

Yes, she could sneak away.
But afterwards, we couldn't.

Menelaos

What are you saying? Your fear of that mob is excessive.

Agamemnon

Khalkas will tell them his prophecy.

Menelaos

A dead man can't tell them anything. I can see to that.

Agamemnon

Prophets, ha!
The only thing they see clearly is their own self-interest.

Menelaos

They're a waste of flesh and blood, that's all.

Agamemnon

But there's someone else we've been forgetting.
Aren't you afraid of him?

Menelaos

I might be if you said his name. I can't read your thoughts.

Agamemnon

The son of Sisyphos. He knows everything that's gone on.

Menelaos

Odysseus? He's neither inclined nor in a position
    to make trouble for us.

Agamemnon

He's shifty . . . and he rides that mob as if it were his horse.

Menelaos

I grant you he's ambitious.
It's an addiction with him . . . a deadly one.

Agamemnon

So can't you see him, pedestaled on a rock,
    with the army pressing on all sides?
Can't you already hear him, revealing the oracles of Kalkhas
    and telling the army how I promised the sacrifice
        demanded by Artemis
    and then went back on my word to her?
Won't he simply wrap the mob's reins in his fist
    and turn its rage on you and me,
        calling on the army to murder us
            and to see to the girl's sacrifice?
Or suppose we do escape and reach home safely . . .
    then the army will march on Argos instead of Troy,
    and it will be our city that will be all ashes and blood.
So now you see why I despair.
My only choice is to endure what happens.
The gods are in control now.
But there is one thing you can do for me, Menelaos.
Go to camp and make sure no one tells Klytemnestra
    anything until my daughter is safe in Hades' arms.
If I am to do this, the last thing I need is an hysterical wife.

Menelaos exits. Agamemnon turns to the Chorus.

And you, women, wherever you're from, be careful.
Say nothing.

Agamemnon goes into his tent.

Chorus

Blessed are those who sip the pleasures of Aphrodite
Slowly, from a shallow cup.
In her bed, peace of mind is a rare prize.
Blessed is anyone who finds calm there,
Where most are driven mad.
Eros, the golden-haired boy with the bow,
Has but two arrows in his quiver.
The one brings bliss.
The other casts a net of confusion
And chaotic pain.
Keep that boy and his arrows,
I beg you, radiant lady,
Far from me and from my bed.
I pray for the middle path,
For a tame love that knows its place.
I want my share of Aphrodite.
But no more.

The race of mortals is a diverse lot.
They go their different ways.
Yet wisdom walks only the road of integrity.
Children, like trees, grow toward the light
If held straight, early on, by a firm hand.
Wisdom begins with reverence
And knows the meaning of shame.
It cleanses the mind,
Enamoring it of truth.
The result is an honorable life,
which lives on forever
In the stories men tell.
Virtue is quarry worthy of a great hunt.
For women it means keeping their lives
And their love secret from the world.
For men it means in myriad ways
The service of their city,
Making it flourish,
Leaving it always greater
With the passing of time.

Paris,
Long ago you were taken to the slopes of Ida
To live among the flocks you kept.
Soon you filled the mountains with your songs,
Barbarian melodies from a Phrygian flute.
From the sound of it, to a wistful ear,
It could have been Olympos.
One day, as your herds grazed,
You gazed upon inhuman beauty
And made a fateful choice,
Propelling you to Greece
To a luxuriant palace and a luxuriant queen.
Your eyes met and made love at once,
In the exchange of a glance.
So, one quarrel has spawned another,
And, with ships and sharpened spears,
Greece makes its way to towering Troy.

*Klytemnestra and Iphigenia approach in their chariot,
escorted by Attendants from Argos.*

Choral Leader

Look, see how generous fortune is to the fortunate.
It runs in their blood.
Here is Iphigenia, daughter of the great king, my mistress.
And Klytemnestra, daughter of Tyndareos, with her son.
They have the blood of kings in them.
When they empty their cup of happiness,
            someone refills it.
The gods themselves, the source of all blessings,
            are barely more blessed than these,
                        the cream of mortals.

Daughters of Khalkis,
            let us stand here where we are,
            and help the great queen down from the chariot,
                        lest she lose her balance and fall.
Here, we offer you our hands,
As strong as they are soft.

31

To Iphigenia and Orestes.

Famed daughter and son of Agamemnon,
   so new to this place, relax. Have no fear.
We too are strangers here.
Calmly, quietly, strangers to strangers, we welcome you.

Klytemnestra

I regard these words of yours,
   so kind and gracious toward us,
      to be a bright omen for this day on which
     I bring my daughter to what I have every hope
       will be a splendid marriage.

To her Argive attendants.

Now if you would first lift down my daughter's dowry
   from the chariot and -- carefully now! --
      bring it into the tent.

To Iphigenia.

Next, my sweet girl,
   lower your delicate feet over the side of the chariot.
Young ladies, take her in your arms and lift her down.

The Chorus assist Iphigenia down from the chariot.

I too will need someone's arm for support,
   if I'm going to get down from here with any dignity.
And someone stand in front of the yoke horses.
They're looking wild and ready to bolt.
Finally, little Orestes, son of Agamemnon.
Lift him down, will you?
He has legs of his own; but they don't do much yet.
O . . . are you still sleeping, little one?
Does the chariot rock you to sleep?
Wake up now, smiling. This is your sister's wedding day!
It's a special day for you, too. You will get a brother-in-law,
   a fine man, in fact nearly a god,
      the grandson of Nereus.

But for now, sit down here by my feet.
Come here, Iphigenia, stand close to me.
Show these young women
        how sweetly blessed I am in you.
Look, look who's coming . . . the father you love so much.

The sound of Agamemnon's footsteps precedes him.

Iphigenia

O mother, don't be upset
        if I run ahead of you to hug him.

Agamemnon emerges from the tent.

Klytemnestra

August lord Agamemnon,
        you summoned us and we have come.

Iphigenia

Father! I long to run to you
        and throw my arms around you.
I've missed you so much!

To Klytemnestra.

Don't be angry with me.

Klytemnestra

It's all right, child.
Of all the children I've borne to your father,
        you've always loved him most.

*Iphigenia runs to her father and clings to him. Then, still
holding his hand, she steps back and looks at him.*

Iphigenia

O father, it has felt like such a long time.
Seeing you makes me so happy!

Agamemnon

You speak for us both.
You make your father happy.

Iphigenia

O yes, be as happy as I am . . . please!
Father you've done such a wonderful thing
        in bringing me here to you.

Agamemnon

You find words where I don't, child.

Iphigenia

Father, I know you're happy to see me;
        but it doesn't show.

Agamemnon

As king and general, I have a lot on my mind.

Iphigenia

Well put it all away somewhere for now.
I want to be your only concern.

Agamemnon

All right. I'm here with you . . . nowhere else.

Iphigenia

Then stop frowning.
Make those furrows go away.

Agamemnon

There. Now you can see how happy you make me, child.

Iphigenia

But now you're crying, father. Why?

Agamemnon

Because there's a long separation ahead for us.

Iphigenia

I don't understand.
O dearest father, I don't know what you mean.

Agamemnon

If you did, I would cry even more.

Iphigenia

Then let's pretend that neither of us knows anything.
Maybe that will help you smile.

Agamemnon

Sighing deeply and speaking to himself.

How much longer can I say nothing?

To Iphigenia.
All right, whatever you say.

Iphigenia

Father, just stay home with us.

Agamemnon

O I wish . . . but I cannot . . . and how painful that is!

Iphigenia

Why can't all the spears in the world be broken in half
and Menelaos' troubles just go away?

Agamemnon

I will be long gone and so will many others
before that happens.

Iphigenia

But you've been away so long already here in Aulis.

Agamemnon

Yes, something prevents us from setting sail.

Iphigenia

Father . . . these "Trojans" everyone is talking about . . .
    where do they live?

Agamemnon

In the city of Priam, the father of Paris.
I wish they didn't exist.

Iphigenia

So you're leaving me, Father, and going far away?

Agamemnon

Just as you are, my child.

Iphigenia

But I want to go with you. Couldn't you take me along?

Agamemnon

You have a journey of your own to make,
    across a different sea.
Don't forget your father there.

Iphigenia

Will I set sail with my mother, or alone?

Agamemnon

Alone, without father or mother.

Iphigenia

So you are making a home for me somewhere else? Where?

36

Agamemnon

That's enough. You're still only a child.
You don't need to know.

Iphigenia

Then finish whatever you need to do in Troy,
    and hurry back to me.

Agamemnon

Before that I must sacrifice a victim, here in Aulis.

Iphigenia

Of course.
The offering of victims to the gods is a sacred duty.
You must see to it.

Agamemnon

We will see to it together.
Your place will be beside the bowl of purifying waters.

Iphigenia

Then, around the altar and its victim . . . will we dance?

Agamemnon

O sweet thing, I would give anything for your innocence.
Now go inside the tent.
Young girls don't belong out in public view.
First, hold my hand and give me a kiss.
Soon you are going away from your father
    for all too long a time.
Your breast and cheeks and golden hair . . . all so soft . . .
Why, on this sweet head, must Helen
    and the walls of Troy come crashing down?
I touch you and the dam within me breaks.

Agamemnon begins weeping uncontrollably.

Run . . . run inside.

To Klytemnestra.

Daughter of Leda, I'm sorry. Excuse this bath of self-pity.
Who would believe that all I'm doing
        is marrying off my daughter to Akhilleus?
It's supposed to be an occasion of joy.
But when a father who has watched over his daughter
      as closely as I have gives her away,
         his joy comes mixed with grief.

Klytemnestra

Do you imagine I don't know that?
How could I find fault with your tears,
      knowing well how I will weep
         when I hear the wedding song
           and lead our little girl away?
But it is what happens, over and over;
      and time will dry our tears.
Now, this man
      to whom you have betrothed our daughter . . .
To be sure, I've heard of him;
      but I'm anxious to hear more.
Tell me where he comes from and about his family.

Agamemnon

I'll begin with Asopos. He had a daughter named Aigina.

Klytemnestra

And who married her? A god or a mortal?

Agamemnon

Zeus did; and she bore him a son Aikos,
      who eventually took Oinone for his wife.

Klytemnestra

And which of the sons of Aiakos became his heir?

38

Agamemnon

Peleus, who then married Thetis,
        the daughter of divine Nereus.

Klytemnestra

Did he do so with the gods' blessing,
        or did he take her by force?

Agamemnon

Zeus himself betrothed her to Peleus.
Then, on the appointed day,
        briny Nereus gave her away.

Klytemnestra

And where did they wed . . . in the depths of the sea?

Agamemnon

No, no. They were married at the foot of Mt. Pelion,
        in a sacred place, where Kheiron makes his home.

Klytemnestra

Was it the same place where they say the centaurs live?

Agamemnon

The same.
It was there the gods made a splendid feast
        for Peleus and his bride.

Klytemnestra

So who reared Akhilleus? His father or his mother?

Agamemnon

Neither did.
Kheiron brought him up to know nothing
        of the weakness and corruption of mortals.

Klytemnestra

So he had a wise teacher in Kheiron,
   and an even wiser father in Peleus,
    who made it all happen.

Agamemnon

And now you know the kind of man
   your daughter is marrying.

Klytemnestra

He will do.
Where in Greece is his city located?

Agamemnon

It lies within the borders of Phthia,
   on the banks of the River Apidanos.

Klytemnestra

Then he will take our daughter there?

Agamemnon

Once she is his, that will be for him to decide.

Klytemnestra

May they flourish together!
What day has been set for their wedding?

Agamemnon

They will marry at the next full moon,
   a bright omen for their life together.

Klytemnestra

Our daughter's pre-nuptial sacrifice to the goddess . . .
   have you seen to that yet?

Agamemnon

I am about to. That's exactly where we are at.

Klytemnestra

And after that, of course, you will hold the wedding feast?

Agamemnon

Yes, after I have made the requisite sacrifice.

Klytemnestra

And where shall I set out the women's meal?

Agamemnon

On the beach, beside the ships.

Klytemnestra

Well, it seems we make do. It should be all right.

Agamemnon

Now, as my wife, do you know what you should do?
Listen to me now, and do as I say.

Klytemnestra

Just say it.
Deferring to you is a habit by now.

Agamemnon

Right.
I shall stand at the wedding
        between the bridegroom and my daugh . . .

Klytemnestra

Interrupting.
You'll do what? You . . . in my place . . . taking my part?

Agamemnon

Along with the army, yes.
We men shall give your daughter away.

Klytemnestra

And where are we women to be while this is going on?

Agamemnon

Where you belong, home in Argos
      minding your other daughters.

Klytemnestra

You expect me to abandon my little girl
      on her wedding day?
Who is going to raise the wedding torch?

Agamemnon

I will provide whatever light suits the bridal pair.

Klytemnestra

You're trampling our customs as if they don't matter.
But they do!

Agamemnon

How customary is it for you, a married woman,
      to stay here among an army of men?

Klytemnestra

I'm the one who brought that girl into the world;
      and I'm going to give her away.
It's only fair.

Agamemnon

How fair is it for our daughters at home
      to be all alone?

Klytemnestra

They aren't alone.
They're safe in their quarters, well looked after.

Agamemnon

Obey me, woman!

Klytemnestra

No.
By the goddess who rules over Argos, I refuse.
You see to your affairs,
        and I will see to mine.
I have a wedding to get ready for.

Klytemnestra enters the tent.

Agamemnon

Sighing audibly in evident confusion and despair.

It's no use.
Wanting her out of the way
        isn't enough to make her leave.
Whatever I try to do, the opposite happens.
But I must go on, sharpening my wits
        against those I love most,
                scheming their ruin.
It is time to meet with Khalkas,
        who has a taste for sacrifice.
In league with him, I must carry out
        something sweet to Artemis and ruinous to me,
        something for which Greece shall pay a heavy price.

This much I know.
A man is better off living alone
        than with a woman who defies him.
Keep a faithful wife or none at all.
That's the rule to be followed.

Agamemnon exits; and the Chorus enters.

Chorus
They will come.
Aboard their thousand ships
Bristling with arms,
The Greeks will swarm to Troy.
To the swirling waters of Simois,
Silver in the sun, to the plains of Ilion,
Cherished by Apollo,
They will come.
Already I hear the cries of Kassandra.
Even now she flings her head,
Crowned with the crisp green leaves of her god,
From side to side, lashing the air
With her wild, knotted golden hair,
As divine lips whisper into her ears
The story of all that must be.

Perched on their walls and towers,
Soon the sons and daughters of Troy
Will stand and stare and wait,
As bronze-clad Ares,
His wooden sea-steeds churning the sea beneath him,
Nears the mouth of Simois.
With all the whetted bronze stacked aboard the ships
Like one giant blade in his hands,
Ares will labor savagely
To return from the city of Priam,
To Greece where she belongs,
Helen, whose twin brothers
Sparkle in the night sky.

Around the towered walls of Troy,
Ares will draw a circle of blood,
Marking out the city for slaughter.
With the king's head hanging from his belt,
He will dismantle Troy stone by stone,
As the women and their sorry queen
Hemorrhage their souls in wails that no one hears.
Helen too will cry out on that day.
Helen, child of Zeus or not,
Will learn to regret the day
She flew her husband's bed.
Never this for me or for my children
Or for theirs!
Never to sit and wait at our looms,
Like the women at Troy,
For the gates of hell to open.

"Who," they whisper to each other,
"Who will wrap my long hair around his fist
And drag me from the ashes
Of everything I know?"
All this, Helen, is your doing!
Who cares now whether the tale is true
That Leda bore you to a swan,
Surrendering to a wild flutter of wings,
The barely hidden frenzy of god,
Or whether Leda and her swan
Are a figment of the Muses,
A story for some other time?
Either way, you bring the same doom.

Chorus exits, and Akhilleus enters.

Akhilleus

Calling into the tent.

Where is the commander of Akhaians?
Will one of his attendants inform him that Akhilleus,
        son of Peleus, stands outside his tent
                and wishes to have a word with him?

45

He should know that this sojourn of ours
                beside the Euripos
                        weighs on each of us differently.
Those of us who are unmarried
                have left behind empty houses,
                        while others have virtually deserted their wives,
                                leaving them childless besides.
All for us to sit on the beach
                and count the weeks go by like clouds.

Yet Greece aches with longing for this war.
The army is feverish with desire.
This is a fire some god has set.

Like anyone else who would present his own case,
                I have a right to speak my mind.
I have forsaken Peleus and our city of Pharsalia,
                only to languish here beside the Euripos,
                        abandoned by the winds.
Meanwhile, day by day, I must placate my Myrmidons.
Their complaints are incessant :
                "Akhilleus," they cry out,
                        "what are we waiting for?"
"How much more of our lives must we waste
                on this so-called invasion of Troy?"
"To hell with the sons of Atreus and their delays.
If there's going to be action, we want to see it now.
Otherwise, lead the army home."

Klytemnestra enters.

Klytemnestra

Child of divine Thetis, I heard your voice,
                and I come to greet you.

Akhilleus

Staring at Klytemnestra and muttering to himself.

O goddess, guardian of modesty,
                who is this exquisite woman before my eyes?

46

Klytemnestra

You have no idea who I am?

Akhilleus shakes his head in response.

Well, that's not surprising.
You've never been in my presence before.
I do appreciate your modesty and respect.

Akhilleus

Who are you?
What is a woman like you doing here in the Greek camp?

Klytemnestra

I am Klytemnestra, the daughter of Leda.
My husband is lord Agamemnon.

Akhilleus

You have said with admirable succinctness . . .
        that I don't belong here.
I am ashamed to have been conversing
        with another man's wife.

Klytemnestra

Wait! Why are you running off?
Give me your hand, a blessed beginning
        to the marriage that will soon be ours.

Akhilleus

What are you saying?
I should touch your hand? It is forbidden!
Doing that would shame me before Agamemnon.

Klytemnestra

Forbidden?
Child of Nereid Thetis, goddess of the seas, since when
        is it forbidden for a mother to hold the hand
                of her daughter's future spouse?

47

Akhilleus

Spouse? What are you talking about?
My lady, you leave me speechless.
You're delirious!
This whole thing is in your head . . . nowhere else.

Klytemnestra

This happens to everyone, you know.
Men always get embarrassed
        when they meet their in-laws for the first time.
It reminds them they're getting married.

Akhilleus

My lady, I'm not, never have been, espoused
        to your daughter.
If I am to marry into the house of Atreus,
        I have not been told.

Klytemnestra

What's happening?
Now I am as confused by your words
        as you have been by mine.

Akhilleus

Between the two of us we'll figure this out.
One of us must be close to the truth.

Klytemnestra

Something quite vicious has been done to me.
I see now that the marriage I've come here to celebrate
        doesn't exist, except as a figment in someone's mind.
Now I am the one who is embarrassed.

Akhilleus

Someone has made a mockery of both of us.
Pay no further attention to it.
Try to let it pass.

Klytemnestra

I've been drawn into someone else's lie . . . shown contempt.
I'm too ashamed to look you in the eye.
Good-bye.

Akhilleus

I know exactly how you feel.
Good-bye.
I'm leaving . . . to look for your husband.

As they turn away from each other, Akhilleus to exit and Klytemnestra to return to the tent, the Old Servant calls to them from a distance and enters as he speaks.

Old Servant

Wait! You, child of a goddess and grandson of Aiakos,
        wait for me.
I would speak with you.

To Klytemnestra, watching him from the door of the tent.

With you too, daughter of Leda.

Akhilleus

Who are you to shout at me like this?
You look and sound distressed.

Old Servant

I am a slave . . . not something I'm proud of . . .
        not something I can change, either.

Akhilleus

Whose slave are you?
Not one of mine . . . not in Agamemnon's camp.

Old Servant

I belong to this lady.
Tyndareos made me part of her dowry.

Akhilleus

Well. I'm here, waiting to learn why you've detained me.
So speak up.

Old Servant

Are you certain there's no one else close enough to hear?

Akhilleus

We are alone.
So come here and speak.

Old Servant

I can only hope that what I know,
      combined with a little luck,
            may yet save those I want to help.

Akhilleus

It sounds as if you know more than we do
      about what is happening.

To Klytemnestra.

This may be important to us.

*The Old Servant, reaching for Klytemnestra's hand, begins to
lower himself to his knees. Klytemnestra impatiently stops
him.*

Klytemnestra

Don't waste time kissing my hand, old one.
Just tell us what you have to say.

Old Servant

You know me, lady. You know how far back
      my loyalty goes to you and your children.

Klytemnestra

I remember that,
> when I was still only a child in my father's house,
> > you were already one of his servants.

Old Servant

Then I came to the house of lord Agamemnon
> as part of your dowry.

Klytemnestra

Yes, you came to Argos with me
> and have belonged to me ever since.

Old Servant

Exactly.
I am loyal to your husband, but more loyal to you.

Klytemnestra

Then tell me about this secret you're keeping.

Old Servant

Your daughter . . . her own father is about to kill her . . .
> himself, with his own hand.

Klytemnestra

What?
I spit out your words, old man!
You're out of your mind.

Old Servant

He will slit the wretched girl's soft pale neck with a knife.

Klytemnestra

*Gasping and struggling to breathe as if every bit of air has
been sucked from her lungs by the Old Servant's words.*

No . . . not this.
You're telling me my husband's gone mad?

51

Old Servant

Only when it comes to you and your girl.
Otherwise he has his wits.

Klytemnestra

Why this?
What demon from hell whispered this in his ear?

Old Servant

If you believe Kalkhas, it is a demon from the gods,
        a condition for the army's arrival.

Klytemnestra

So my husband is after my little girl with a knife.
Iphigenia . . . you and I . . .
Arrival? Arrival where?

Old Servant

Troy. Menelaos wants Helen back.

Klytemnestra

And my girl is the price of her homecoming.
Iphigenia for Helen.
Is this what they're calling "destiny"?

Old Servant

You've said it, word for word. She will soon be a gift,
        to Artemis from your husband.

Klytemnestra

My daughter's marriage . . .
            that was his way of getting me to send her here . . .
                    far from her home . . . and from me?
Old Servant

He knew that you would be only too glad
        to give up your daughter to Akhilleus' bed.

52

Klytemnestra

Iphigenia . . . you and I were in such a hurry . . .
      running toward the void!

Old Servant

What you two must suffer breaks my heart;
      but what Agamemnon does
          terrifies my soul.

Klytemnestra

Then it's done.
I . . . I . . . I can't even stop my own tears!

Old Servant

It's time for tears, when you lose a child.

Klytemnestra

All this you've been telling me, old one . . .
      where did you say you learned it from?

Old Servant

From a tablet I was taking to you,
      a second tablet from your husband.

Klytemnestra

Reaffirming his demand
      that I lead my daughter to her deathbed,
          or was he having second thoughts?

Old Servant

He was telling you not to send Iphigenia.
He was at the time thinking as a husband . . . and a father.

Klytemnestra

So you were carrying that word to me . . .
Why didn't I ever receive it?

Old Servant

Menelaos is to blame.
He stopped me and took away the tablet.

Klytemnestra

To Akhilleus.

Grandson of Nereus, child of Peleus,
      have you heard all this?

Akhilleus

Every word of your misery and of the part I've played in it.
I take none of it lightly.

Klytemnestra

With you and your bed as bait,
      they would lead my girl to slaughter.

Akhilleus

Your husband will answer to me . . .
      not just for his abuse of my name.

Klytemnestra falls to her knees in supplication before Akhilleus.

Klytemnestra

As I am simply mortal, and you spring from a divine womb,
      I feel no shame in falling before you
            and clasping your knees in supplication.
What good are the airs to me now?
My daughter matters more than my pride.
Child of divine Thetis,
      champion me and the girl they call your wife.
Save us . . . as if their story were true.
I did, after all, bring her for your wedding.
Now I see I must give her over to slaughter.
If you do nothing to stop this,
      your name will go dark forever.

54

You may not have a bond with that poor girl,
          but all the same, on the world's lips,
                    you are her dear, devoted spouse.
By your beard . . . by your right hand . . .
          by your divine mother, I beg you!
You must save us!
It was your name that brought us here . . . to this.
Your knee is the last altar to which I can run.
You are the only sanctuary I have left.
Here in this place I have no one on my side.
You know all about Agamemnon,
          my husband turned animal.
You see what I am, a woman alone in the camp of men,
          more like a mob than an army,
                    blood in their eyes already . . .
          all very useful and encouraging, I imagine,
                    when its on your side.
If you would dare to lift your hand and your sword for us,
          then we will be saved. If not, we are lost.

Choral Leader

Motherhood is a strange, powerful thing, a great love charm,
          giving this much in common to all women:
                    there is nothing they will not do or endure
                    for their children.

Akhilleus

Lady, these words of yours, like a brisk wind,
          lift the fire in my soul to full flame.
In grief and in joy, in the worst and in the brightest of times,
          I know all about moderation.
I know what it means to walk a thin righteous line in my life,
          selling my soul to no one.
I know that such a life is possible for any mortal,
          who thinks his way carefully day by day.
There are times, of course, for thinking less,
          when it is sweet to let the mind drift,
                    just as there are times for heavy thought,
          when reason is the best rule.

From Kheiron, the most reverent of men,
      my teacher in all things,
            I learned to live these and other simple truths.
Now, as for the sons of Atreus,
      I shall follow them when their commands are just,
            and ignore them when they are not.
I bring to Troy, as to everywhere else, a free spirit;
      and my spear will make the war god proud, always.

Lady, beaten down savagely
      by those who ought to love you most,
            my youth and my strength, such as they are,
      are yours, a wall of compassion thrown around you.
Never, so long as I stand, will your daughter,
      my so-called bride,
            die a victim at her father's hand.
Your father will have to spin his deadly web without me.
No more will my name be the bladeless sword
      that slays your girl.
Let your husband drink the cup he poured.
I would smell the guilt on me forever,
      if your sweet, unsullied girl suffered hideous abuse
      and went to an unthinkable end because of me . . .
            all because she rushed to be my bride.
How does something, someone, so precious
      become nothing?
I do wonder about that.

I would be the shabbiest of Greeks,
      a thin nothing like Menelaos . . .
I would be the son not of Peleus
      but of some nameless outcast,
            if I let my name do your husband's butchery.

By my grandfather Nereus,
      nursed in the arms of the heaving sea,
            lord Agamemnon will not so much as touch
      the hem of your daughter's robe.
And for the prophet Kalkhas, waiting with his lustral waters,
      there will be a bitter surprise.

56

What are prophets anyway?
Nothing but liars playing the odds.
When they're lucky, they get a few things right.
When they don't, they disappear.

Let me clarify one thing now, for the record.
I'm not after your daughter.
I have more women after me than Agamemnon has ships.
For me it is a matter of rage, not love.
Lord Agamemnon has done me an outrageous wrong!
If he wants to use my name to trap his daughter,
        he must ask me first.
It was my name more than anything else
        that persuaded Klytemnestra
                to hand over her daughter to Agamemnon.
If my name were enough
        to send the Greeks on their way to Troy,
                it would be theirs . . . for the *asking*.
I would not deny my fellow men-in-arms
        what is for our common good.
But now, apparently, I am nothing,
        someone for my fellow warlords to humor or abuse
                at their whim.

Drawing his sword.

You see this sword.
Long before it sees action in Troy,
        it will know the stain and taste of slaughter,
                if anyone tries to take your daughter.
So, put your heart at rest.
Think of me as a god, capable of anything,
        come to your side.
Of course, at the moment,
        I am not a god.
It is something I will have to become.

Choral Leader

Child of Peleus, your words are worthy of you,
        worthy too of your mother Thetis,
                sublime goddess of the seas.

57

Klytemnestra

Speechless at first, groping for words.

Where among the words I know
      am I to find the praise you deserve?
Without saying too little and losing your good-will.
    I think few words are best
          for I know that men of your character
    have a way of despising
        those who lavish them with praise.

I am ashamed to parade my afflictions before you.
What I suffer is, after all, my concern.
My pain is not contagious. You cannot catch it from me.
All the same,
      it is the way of decent, feeling men like you
         to reach out to those in misery
    and to do what can be done for them.
Pity me and my daughter.
Surely by now we are pitiable.
I see now that having you as my son-in-law was a mirage,
      wishful thinking, nothing more.
The bright day will come, Akhilleus,
        when you wish to take a wife.
Be careful now.
My daughter's death could cast a long shadow.
You spoke well, just now, from start to finish.
I know that, if you will it, my child shall be saved.

So what now? Would you like my daughter
      to cling to your knees as a suppliant?
Of course that would hardly be fitting at her age.
All the same, if that is what you want,
      she will come to you, all ablush no doubt,
        looking every way but yours.
Yet, if I can win from you what we need,
      without her being here,
        then let her remain inside.
She is very modest,
      something I try as best I can to respect.

58

Akhilleus

Lady, I would rather you didn't bring your daughter
     into my sight.
We would only inspire some mindless scandal.
The vast armies assembled here,
     stranded far from their homes,
     have nothing better to do than to tell sordid stories.
The filthier the better for them.
It makes no difference at all
     whether your daughter comes to supplicate my help.
Only one great issue concerns me now;
     and that is averting your doom.
Now that you've heard that, know one more thing:
     I don't know how to lie.
I would die before I would mock you with a string of lies.
Unless your daughter lives through this,
     my own life is nothing to me.

Klytemnestra

Bless you for helping us in our need.
May you know lasting happiness.

Akhilleus

But for the present, so that it might go well,
     you must listen to me carefully.

Klytemnestra

What is it? I'm listening.

Akhilleus

We must work on your husband . . .
     talk him back to sanity.

Klytemnestra

He may be beyond that.
His fear of the army eats him alive.

59

Akhilleus

You can change anyone's mind with the right words.

Klytemnestra

I hope we don't have to depend on that.
But just tell me what I must do.

Akhilleus

First do this. On your knees, beg him not to kill your child.
If that doesn't work, then you must come to me.
But if he listens and does as you ask,
            then there is no need to involve me further;
                        for your deliverance is assured.
If your well-being can be achieved with words alone,
            without resort to force, it is all the better for us both.
Besides, once the army turns on me,
            there will be less I can do for you.
So, this is our first plan, in which I play no part.
If it succeeds, you and those you love will know great joy.

Klytemnestra

It seems a good plan. I am willing to do what you think best.
But if something goes wrong and I fail,
            where will I see you again? Where?
If I am desperate and need your strong arm
            to ward off disaster, where do I go?
Where can I find you?

Akhilleus

You won't need to. It is for me to watch over you;
            and that is what I intend to do.
I will be there, at the right place, when you need me.
I would not want anyone to see you in a panic,
            thrashing your way through a mob of men.
Don't do anything like that to shame your father's house.
Tyndareos is a great man in Greece. He deserves better
            than to hear the kind of stories you would provoke.

60

Klytemnestra
All right, then. I am yours to command. Tell me what to do.
You are a just man.
If the gods exist at all, you will flourish.
If they don't, why should we care. . . about anything?

Akhilleus exits as Klytemnestra enters the tent. Next the Chorus enters.

Chorus
Listen . . .
Flutes carved form black lotus wood,
Dance-enchanted lyres,
The shrill frenzy of reed pipes . . .
Imagine the sounds,
The wedding-song
To Peleus and his bride.
With golden sandals strapped to their feet
And their lustrous hair billowing in the breeze,
The divine Muses,
Climbed the slopes of Peleion
To a feast set by gods.
Above the rhythm of their steps
The gracious daughters of Zeus
Lifted their song,
A hymn of praise to Thetis
And to the son of Aiakos,
A hymn that flew over the mountains of the centaurs
And danced through the forests of Pelion.

61

Then the child of Dardanos,
Phrygian Ganymede,
The bud of joy in Zeus' bed,
Poured a gleaming libation
Into the hollow of a golden bowl,
While down below on the sea's edge
Fifty sparkling daughters of Nereus,
Slipped loose from the waters
And danced in a circle on the salt-white sand,
A wedding-dance for Peleus
And his bride from the sea.

Then of a sudden,
Waving lances of stripped pine
And wearing crowns
Of recklessly woven leaves,
A band of misbehaving centaurs
Hoofed into the feast
And gathered around the bowl of Bakkhos,
Brimming with wine.
In one voice they offered a thunderous toast.
"Hail, daughter of Nereus.
We have it straight from Kheiron, our seer,
On Apollo's word,
That you will bear a son
To be a light to all of Thessaly.
One day he will lead his Myrmidons,
Armed to the teeth,
To the far-famed land of Priam,
Leaving only ashes behind.
He will wear armor
Forged in the flames of Hephaistos,
Armor glinting with hammered gold,
A gift from you, Thetis,
The mother who bore him."
So the gods and their guests
Sang wedding songs to noble Peleus and his bride,
First among the daughters of Nereus,
Proclaiming theirs to be a marriage
Made in the stars, lucky and blessed.

But to you, child,
We sing a different song.
On your soft lovely hair,
Argive warriors will set a crown
Of a different sort,
Suited to the brow of some unblemished calf,
Led by the neck from the mountain cave
To sacrifice.
You too will have your neck cut
Wide and deep,
Child,
You were not raised on some wild mountain slope
To the tune of a herdsman's pipe,
But raised in a palace,
Washed and veiled by your mother,
To be a bride for kings,
What becomes of shame?
When corruption wears the crown?
When mortals turn from decency
And chaos climbs the throne,
When the fellowship of men
In the fear of god
Is a forgotten fancy,
How many more deaths can virtue die?

Klytemnestra enters and looks in several directions, scanning the distance. She addresses the Chorus.

Klytemnestra

I've come out to look for my husband.
It's been quite a while now since he left this tent
and went off somewhere.
In the meantime my poor child has learned
of the death her father plans for her.
Soaked with her own tears,
she screams until her voice gives out,
and then sobs quietly
until she has the strength to scream again.

Klytemnestra sees Agamemnon approaching.

Speaking of Agamemnon . . .
I no more than mention his name,
     and he comes running . . . to his moment of truth.
It is time to cast some light on the atrocity he arranges
     against his daughter.

Agamemnon

Daughter of Leda, I'm so glad to find you here,
     outside the tent,
  where I can tell you something,
     away from Iphigenia,
  something a bride-to-be shouldn't hear.

Klytemnestra

So you've stumbled on the perfect moment
     for saying something.
I wonder what it is.

Agamemnon

I want you to go in and send the girl out here,
     to accompany her father.
Everything stands ready for the pre-nuptial sacrifice:
     the purifying waters,
     the barley grains for throwing into the cleansing fire,
     the young, perfect victims, whose dark blood
     will spray the goddess Artemis and make her glad.

Klytemnestra

When put that way, it sounds so official . . . so correct.
That's what words can do.
But deeds are different . . . especially yours.
I have no words at all for them.

Calling into the tent.

Come out here, child; for you already know everything
     about your father and his ambitions for you.
And bring with you your brother Orestes.
Wrap him gently in your robe.

Iphigenia enters with Orestes.

See, here she is, your little girl,
      who doesn't know how to displease you.
So I intend to speak for her . . . and for myself.

Agamemnon

To Iphigenia.

Child, why are you crying?
Why don't you look at me . . . give me a smile?
Why stare at the ground,
      and cover your eyes with your robe?

Klytemnestra

One word could tell my story, beginning, middle, and end:
      pain.
Maybe two: betrayal.
So where do I start?

Agamemnon

What is this . . . all of you looking at me the same way,
      with such confusion and anguish in your eyes?

Klytemnestra

Husband, I'm going to ask you an honest question.
I'd like an honest answer.

Agamemnon

There's no need to be confrontational.
I'm happy to answer your question.

Klytemnestra

It's about my daughter here, yours too . . .
Are you hoping to kill her?

Agamemnon is, at first, unable to speak. He makes sounds, but no words.

Agamemnon

What a perverse, reckless thing to say!
You have no right even to think . . .

Klytemnestra

Relax . . . and answer my question.

Agamemnon

Ask a reasonable question and you'll get a reasonable answer.

Klytemnestra

I have only one question. Answer it.

Agamemnon

It's fate . . . destiny . . . they've come for me.
They are divine, and I am only human.

Klytemnestra

You mean, they've come for us.
We are lost.

Agamemnon

What . . . what has happened to you?

Klytemnestra

You can stand there and ask me that?
You must have mislaid your wits.

There is a long, tense silence, in which Agamemnon sighs all but inaudibly.

Agamemnon

To himself.

It's all over.
I've been found out.

Klytemnestra

Look, I know the whole story.
I've learned exactly what you intend to do to me.
Besides, your silence and your sighs are as eloquent
        as any confession you could make.
Still, you might as well say something on your behalf.

Agamemnon

I think not. Silence will do.
Telling lies at this point would only add shame
        to my misfortune.

Klytemnestra

Now you hear me. No more riddles.
I'm going to drag the truth out here where we can see it.
To be orderly about this, I'll begin in the beginning.
First things first . . . courtship.
You'll remember I was not the most willing bride.
After you murdered my husband, Tantalos,
        and tore our tiny babe from my breast,
                shattering its head against the nearest wall,
        then you took me . . . not without help.

But then . . . the unexpected.
My two brothers, the twin sons of Zeus,
        appeared at your door, on horseback.
Even in the midday sun, they glistened like stars.
Behind them marched an army, on my behalf.
It took no time for you to find your knees,
        crawling to my father, Tyndareos,
                who took pity on your neck and saved it.
So once again I was yours.

In time, I came around to you and your house.
In fact -- there's not denying it -- I became the ideal wife:
        loving, faithful, competent.
I kept the kind of house you could leave with peace of mind
        and return to with joy.

Inane, useless women practically grow on trees.
But the kind of woman you had is a rare catch.
I bore you this son and three daughters,
of which you are allowing me to keep two.
Somehow I don't feel grateful.
Tell me . . . if someone, anyone, were to ask you
why you are murdering this girl,
what would you say? Tell me.

Silence.

Must I put words in your mouth?
"So that Menelaos can get Helen back."
A lovely, perfect girl for a rotten whore . . .
no one can accuse you of driving a hard bargain.
So we give what we love most for what we despise!

Let me give you something to think about.
Suppose you do go out on this war of yours,
leaving me to mind the house,
and suppose you're away, over there, for a long time,
what do you think will happen to my . . .
disposition?
For instance, when I see her empty chair, her empty room . . .
when everywhere I look, she is gone . . .
when I sit alone and weep,
bleeding from a wound that won't heal. . .
I can hear myself crying out to the girl who isn't there.
"It was your father, the man who planted your seed.
Your own father killed you, child, with his own hand . . .
no one else, no other hand but his."
Do you have a picture yet of what you will leave behind . . .
in your own house?
How much of an excuse, a pretext, will we need,
your remaining children and I,
to prepare for you
the kind of homecoming you deserve?
For god's sake, Agamemnon, don't force me
to become evil . . . to do evil to you!

*Klytemnestra breaks momentarily, and then steels herself for
a second assault.*

After you've sacrificed your girl,
     what are your prayers going to sound like?
What sort of blessing
     does a child-slaughterer like you ask for?
When you go off leaving a trail of shame,
     will you not come home reeking?
And how is it any more fitting for me
     to beg the gods to bless you?
Wouldn't we as much as call the gods idiots,
     if we were to ask blessings
          for those who murder our children?
When you come back to Argos, do you imagine yourself
     falling at the feet of your children . . . apologizing?
Would the gods permit such a farce?
Or, for that matter, which of your children
     would even look at you, knowing that you
          could just as easily murder one of them?
Do you have thoughts like this on your own?
Or do you only fancy yourself in front of armies,
     flaunting your sceptre?
Why not demand a little fairness from your fellow-Greeks?
Put it to them this way: "Greek warriors,
     do you want to sail to Troy?
     Then cast lots to see whose child must die."
That would be the fair way. But no, you volunteer
     your own child instead, to shed "first blood"
          for this vile war of yours.
Why not Hermione, for her own mother's sake?
Why doesn't Menelaos cut his own girl's throat?
If he's made a mess, let him wipe it up.
I'm the faithful wife, the one who *hasn't* defiled
     her husband's bed. Yet I am the one
     to lose my child, while she -- I know it --
          will eventually return to Sparta,
          find her own child flourishing,
     and then live happily ever after.
If anything I've said is off the mark, correct me.
If not, then crawl back to your senses, now.
Change your mind.
Don't kill our girl!

69

Choral Leader

Give way, Agamemnon. Together save your child.
Nothing could be more fair.
No one in the world could disapprove.

Iphigenia

Slowly approaching Agamemnon.

Father, if I had the voice of Orpheus and could charm
        even the hearts of stones with my songs,
    I would sing to you now to make you love me.
But, as I am, I have nothing to add to my words but tears.
I will do my best with them.
Like the suppliant's olive branch, torn from its tree,
    I wrap my body around your knees.
I beg for life with the body you once made to live.
Don't make me die before my time.
Don't force me into the world below
    to stare forever at shadows,
        when I love so much the simple light of day.

I was the first to call you "father."
When you called out "child" for the first time,
    you were calling me.
I was the first little thing to make its nest on your knees.
I remember how sweetly we held and loved each other, and
    how you used to ask me: "What do think, my little one?
Will you grow up one day and marry?
Will I find you happy in your husband's house,
    flourishing as my daughter deserves?"
And then, gripping your beard
    as tightly as my little fist could, as I do now,
        I used to answer:
    "And do you know what I will do for you then, Father,
        when you are old and gray?
    I will throw wide the doors of my house to you,
        and somehow repay you with my love
        for all that you went through for me
    when I was little and needed you."
All this I remember, and all this you forget.

Instead, you want to kill me.
Don't, Father!
For the sake of Pelops and your father Atreus . . .
         For my mother's sake . . . Don't!
My birth was pain enough for her.
Why must she endure my death?
What does the marriage of Helen and Paris
         have to do with me?
How does what they did add up to my ruin?
Father, look at me. Look me in the eyes.
Kiss me.
Give me something sweet to remember as I go to my death,
         something besides your silence to all I say.

To Orestes.

Little brother, wanting to help but so helpless,
         here, go down on your knees with me
               and cry for your father.
With your tears you can beg him not to kill your sister.
You see, when evil and death are near,
         even a tiny child knows it and is afraid.

Father, look at your little boy.
He says nothing, but you can see that he is pleading with you.
Have pity on me. Let me live.
Both of us, together, your oldest and your youngest,
         implore you . . .
Father, I am running out of words.
A few more will say everything.

To look upon the light of day is for all of us the sweetest joy.
In the dark world below there is nothing.
To pray for death is sheer madness.
To be alive, in whatever lowly condition, is better
         than to die a glorious death.

Choral Leader

O hateful Helen, because of you and your bed,
         the house of Atreus splits open and devours itself,
               one member at a time.

71

Agamemnon

I am not blind.
I can see for myself where pity is appropriate
        and where it is not.
I love my children.
I would be deranged if I did not.

To Klytemnestra.

Woman, it is a strange and dreadful thing to be daring
        what I am about to do.
Yes, but no more strange and dreadful than to refuse.
I must . . .

To Iphigenia.

You've seen the army, the ships . . . beyond counting.
You've seen how many kings are assembled here,
        their bronze armor polished for battle.
Yet not one ship, not one warrior, will sail to towering Troy,
        unless I sacrifice you.
The prophecies of Kalkhas are clear on this.
There is no other way for us to mount
        the famed heights of Troy and tear them down.
It is as if Aphrodite has been in every tent, lighting fires.
The army is mad with desire . . .
        the desire to sail at once against the barbarians,
        the desire to put a final end
                to the plundering of Greek beds.
If I ignore the prophecies and deny Artemis your sacrifice,
        the army will start by killing you and me
        and then go on to Argos to kill your sisters there.

Child, I assure you, what Menelaos wants is irrelevant.
I serve Greece, not him.
And Greece demands that I sacrifice you.
My own wishes count for nothing.
You and I are both pawns in this affair.
Child, Greece yearns to be free,
        free once and for all from barbarians,
                who would do their hunting in our beds.
It is for you and for me to do our part.

72

Agamemnon exits. The Choral Leader brings Orestes into the tent.

Klytemnestra

My child . . . women . . . it's hopeless.

To Iphigenia.

Your father has already given you away to Hades.
And, being the kind of man he is,
      he walks out on you besides.

Iphigenia

O, Mother,
      the same song of fate and loss
          comes to your lips and mine.
The radiance of day gives way to unending night.
I belong now to darkness.

O, Paris,
      one day long ago, in a wintry field, far from here,
      you lay alone, Priam's infant son, abandoned,
          left to die, sucking the sky for milk,
              your mother nowhere near,
      only the cold, silent slopes of Ida watching overhead.
"Paris of Ida" they call you now in Troy.
"Paris of Ida" -- named for your fateful mountain.

O, Mother,
      if only the cowherd had never found him there,
      never brought him up, never made a herdsman of him,
          with cattle of his own,
      grazing by crystal-clear springs,
          where the Nymphs dwell,
              in a lush green meadow
                ablaze with hyacinths and roses,
     luring goddesses to come and pick them.

But they did.

73

Pallas Athena came, and Aphrodite with all her wiles,
  and Hera . . . Hermes, too, their escort from Zeus.
Tangled in strife, the three came to Ida quarreling,
  to do battle with their beauty.
It was a contest of their charms:
  Aphrodite offering luxuriance, the sating of desire;
  Athena offering might, the conquest of enemies;
  Hera, consort of lord Zeus,
    offering the splendor of kingship.
I tell you that day's judgment meant glory for Greece,
  and death for me.
I am to be the price of Troy paid on the altar of Artemis.
O Mother, my father who gave me life has fathered my ruin,
  walked out on me, left me alone with his betrayal.
Helen, hapless Helen, like a hateful spectre you haunt me,
  embittering each step I take toward my own murder,
  a victim, not for a wedding, but for a war.
My blood will never wash away, an impious mark
  on an impious man, my own father.

If only Aulis had never opened the haven of its harbor
    to the bronze-beaked ships,
  whose fir-wood hulls will haul an army to Troy.
If only Zeus had never sent the winds that brought them here
  to the banks of Euripos.
What are the winds but the breath of Zeus;
  what drives them but his will?
Mortals long for him to fill their sails and their hearts.
To some he brings fair sailing; on others he breathes doom.
One man sets out and another reaches port,
  while others only wait in stillness.
Unseen, implacable, his breath carries the force of fate.

Mortal life appears to pass in a day,
  until we count our sufferings.
In the shortest life,
  there is always time to endure something more,
    to have one more thing go wrong.
Daughter of Tyndareos, all of Greece labors and suffers
  under the weight of your sin.

Choral Leader

My heart goes out to you in this dark time.
You deserve none of this.

Iphigenia

Seeing the army approaching at a distance.

Mother! Mother, I see a mob of men coming.

Klytemnestra

And I see the son of divine Thetis, Akhilleus,
        for whom you came here.

Iphigenia

To the Chorus

Women, hold open the tent for me,
        so that I can run inside and hide.

Klytemnestra

Child, why run from Akhilleus?

Iphigenia

I am ashamed to meet him.

Klytemnestra

Why?

Iphigenia

Because of the disaster our marriage has become.
I'm embarrassed.

Klytemnestra

In our situation, embarrassment is a luxury we cannot afford.
Stay here. Modesty can wait.
We have things to do.

Akhilleus enters.

Akhilleus

Daughter of Leda, woman of sorrows . . .

Klytemnestra

Yes. I am surely that.

Akhilleus

The army . . . you can hear them . . .
    they've begun to shout and won't stop.

Klytemnestra

What are they shouting about? Tell me.

Akhilleus

About your daughter.

Klytemnestra

You've said enough for me to think the worst.

Akhilleus

They are calling for her sacrifice.

Klytemnestra

Is there no voice on the other side?

Akhilleus

There was mine. I barely escaped.

Klytemnestra

Barely escaped what?

Akhilleus

Being stoned.

76

Klytemnestra

For trying to save my girl?

Akhilleus

Exactly.

Klytemnestra

Who would dare lay a hand on you?

Akhilleus

The whole Greek army.

Klytemnestra

Your own army of Myrmidons . . . aren't they at your side?

Akhilleus

No, they are at my throat.

Klytemnestra

To Iphigenia.
Then we are lost, child.

Akhilleus

They mocked me, saying that I was love-sick.

Klytemnestra

How did you answer them?

Akhilleus

I said they would never kill my bride . . .

Klytemnestra

Right!

Akhilleus

. . . the bride promised to me by her father.

Klytemnestra

And brought from Argos by her mother.

Akhilleus

But they shouted me down.

Klytemnestra

A mob is an evil and terrifying thing.

Akhilleus

I will protect you.

Klytemnestra

One against so many?

Two men approach carrying Akhilleus' armor.

Akhilleus

See. These men bring my armor.

Klytemnestra

May you find the strength you need.

Akhilleus

I will.

Klytemnestra

Then my child will not be sacrificed?

Akhilleus

Not as long as I am here.

Klytemnestra

Who is it that will come and try to take her?

Akhilleus

Odysseus for one; behind him . . . thousands.

Klytemnestra

Odysseus, the son of Sisyphos?

Akhilleus

Yes, the same.

Klytemnestra

Has he taken it to himself to lead the army,
      or did the mob choose him?

Akhilleus

He was elected, as he wanted to be.

Klytemnestra

Elected to murder a child.
It's some office he holds.

Akhilleus

I'll stop him.

Klytemnestra

But he will try to drag her away by force?

Akhilleus

By her golden hair. Yes, of course he'll try.

Klytemnestra

What must I do?

Akhilleus

You must not let go of her.

Klytemnestra

And if I don't, she won't be sacrificed.

Akhilleus

It comes down to that.

Iphigenia

Mother, listen to me,
 this wild rage of yours against your husband . . .
 it's pointless. I see that now.

None of us find it easy to be helpless.

Gesturing toward Akhilleus.

This extraordinary man, our new friend,
 deserves our praise and thanks
 for his willingness to help us.
But you must see to it that he does not incur the army's anger.
That would only imperil him and do nothing for us.

Hear me, Mother, hear what has occurred to me
 and what I have in mind to do.
I have imagined my death and all is well.
I want to shine when I die.
I want nothing to do with anything craven or cheap.
Think about it, Mother, and you will see that I am right.
At this very moment, Greece, in all its might and splendor,
 turns to me.
If the fleet is to set sail, if Troy is to fall,
 if Greek women are once and for all to be secure
 in the happiness of their homes,
 never again prey to barbarians,
 if the spoiling of Helen by Paris
 is to be fully avenged,
 then I must die.

For all of these things are in my hands today.
I alone can set Greece free; and, if I do that,
        my story will be told forever.
Mother, I must not clutch my life too tightly.
After all, you bore me for Greece, not just for yourself.
Thousands of our men have taken up their shields
        and gone to sea,
        to right a wrong done to their fatherland.
Each one of those thousands is ready to kill
        or be killed for Greece.
Who am I, with my one life, to stand in their way?
How could that be right?
How would I explain it to them?

I have one more thing to say.
It would be a waste for this one man
        to take on the whole Greek army
                and to die for the sake of a woman.
Better that a thousand women should give their lives
        to save one man.
Mother, if Artemis wants my life, can I deny her,
        when she is divine and I am only human?

Besides, I am alone against an army of men.
I am without recourse.
So I give my life to Greece.
Sacrifice me and lay waste to Troy.
Long from now, the memory of these events will make up for
        the marriage and the children I never had.
My life will be summed up and preserved in them.
Mother, it is only right and natural
        for Greeks to rule barbarians,
                never the other way around;
        for all they know is slavery, and we are free.

Choral Leader

Child, your nobility is luminous.
It is your fate and the goddess who decreed it
        that are all wrong.

81

Akhilleus

Child of Agamemnon, if somehow you could be my wife,
  it would reveal that one of the gods
     is eager for my happiness.
As it is, you belong to Greece; and I envy you both.
Your words are a thing of beauty, worthy of the fatherland.
You could never have won the battle
  you were about to wage.
Mortals are no match for the gods; so, instead,
  you've resolved to walk the line of the possible
     with all the dignity you can muster.
And yet, when I stand here, listening to you
  and gazing upon your exquisite nature,
     I can't help myself.
I want you more and more for my wife.
Your nobility is almost more than I can bear.
You see, I want to save you.
I want to take you away to my home.
Thetis, be my witness . . .
  I don't know if I will be able to live with myself,
     unless I battle the Greek army to save you.
Remember . . . death is an awful thing.
And it is forever.

Iphigenia

What I say now comes from a place beyond all fear.
Let Helen be the one to send men blithely off to battle,
  to kill or be killed for her body and its charms.
From you, dear friend, I ask something different.
Take no one's life on my account;
  and please, please, don't die for me.
Let me save Greece, if it can be saved.

Akhilleus

Your resolve is extraordinary.
I have nothing to add to what you've said,
  as your mind is made up.

82

Your nobility of soul is a simple truth
      no one can deny or diminish.
Nonetheless, you may change your mind.
Don't forget my offer.
I am going now to lay my weapons near the altar.
I want to prevent your death, not take part in it.
Even when you see the blade near your throat,
      I can still make good my promise to you,
          if you permit me.
If you're being impetuous now,
      I won't let it cost your life.
So, I am off, fully-armed, to the altar of Artemis,
      where I will hold my breath
              and wait for you.

Exit Akhilleus.

Iphigenia
Mother, you have no words but so many tears.
Why weep for me?

Klytemnestra
My despair and my pain are reason enough.

Iphigenia
Oh stop. I need your help to be strong.
Please do as I say.

Klytemnestra

Child, what could I possibly refuse you?
Tell me what you want.

Iphigenia

I want you not to mourn.
Don't cut your hair or wear black for me.

Klytemnestra

Why do you ask this? Aren't I losing you?

Iphigenia

No, not really. I will be saved not lost.
I will win everlasting fame for us both.

Klytemnestra

How can you ask me not to grieve for you?

Iphigenia

What place is there for grief when there will be no tomb?

Klytemnestra

You confuse me. No tomb for the dead?
Will that not enrage the gods?

Iphigenia

The altar of Artemis, daughter of Zeus,
    will mark my grave forever.

Klytemnestra

Your words ring true. I will do as you say, child.

Iphigenia

I will not be forgotten. Nor will anyone ever forget
    how lucky I was to serve Greece.

84

Klytemnestra

Do you have a message for your sisters?

Iphigenia

Only that they should not wear black for me.

Klytemnestra

Do you have some last word for them, from your heart?

Iphigenia

Good-bye.
Mother, take care of Orestes for me.
Make a tall, strong man of him.

Klytemnestra

You must look at him and hold him tight one last time.

Klytemnestra gestures to one of the Chorus to fetch Orestes from the tent, which she does.

Iphigenia

To Orestes, as he enters.

O my sweetest, you did your very best to save your sister.

Iphigenia holds tightly, and then lets go of him.

Klytemnestra

Child, when I go back to Argos, what else can I do for you?

Iphigenia

Don't hate him . . . my father, your husband.

Klytemnestra

He will pay for your death.
Hell will come as a relief to him.

Iphigenia

But he too suffers my loss against his will.
It is all for Greece.

Klytemnestra

Even his lies?
That man betrayed me and disgraced his own house.

Iphigenia

Who will lead me to the altar,
        before they drag me away by my hair?

Klytemnestra

I will. I will be with you.

Iphigenia

No. That's not a good idea.

Klytemnestra

Just to hold your gown.

Iphigenia

Mother, for my sake, listen. Stay here.
It will be better for both of us.
One of father's men can take me to the meadow of Artemis,
        where I will be sacrificed.

Klytemnestra

Child, are you going now?

Iphigenia

Never to return.

Klytemnestra

Leaving your mother?

Iphigenia

All before your eyes.
It feels wrong . . .

Klytemnestra

Wait, don't leave me!

Klytemnestra breaks down, weeping.

Iphigenia

There will be no tears.
Women, sing with me a hymn of praise
  to Artemis, child of Zeus,
      for me and for my day of destiny.
Let holy silence descend upon the host of men.
Let the sacrifice begin.
The baskets and the barley cakes . . . someone bring them.
Let the sacred cleansing fire be lit and blaze forth.
Now, Father, go to the altar and walk around it.
I am coming, with victory in my hands,
      a gift for Greece.
I am coming. I bring salvation.

Women, lead me on . . .
I who will bring down the walls of Phrygian Troy.
Place on my head the wedding crown.
Weave into my hair garlands of victory.
Spatter me with holy waters
      to make me new and pure.
Around the sacred place of Artemis,
      Artemis, our blessed queen . . . around her altar . . .
          lift up your hearts and dance!
For with my blood, spilled out in sacrifice,
      I will answer the gods' demands and set Greece free.

The Chorus crowns Iphigenia with a wedding crown. They form a procession with her to the altar of Artemis. The scene changes to the sacred grove of Artemis, the place of sacrifice.

Choral Leader

O great mother, mistress of us all,
       we will keep our tears to ourselves.
In your holy place, we must show only joy.

Iphigenia

Women, join with me in celebration.
Sing to Artemis, mistress of Aulis,
       whose shrine faces east toward Khalkis,
          across the narrow straits
     where a thousand ships wait.
In my name, they will have their war.
Oh Argos, mother to me . . . Mykene, my home!

Choral Leader

Child, is it to the city of Perseus that you cry out,
       the city whose walls the cyclops toiled to build?

Iphigenia

You brought me into the light, gave me life, for Greece.
So I die for Greece, with no regret.

Choral Leader

Your name and your story will never die.

Iphigenia

O splendorous light of day, that gladdens even the heart
       of god . . . and mine, too . . . good-bye.
I must begin another life, in another place,
       and let the fates weave something new for me.

88

Chorus

See what I see:
The child who would drown Troy in her blood.
Sprinkled with holy water
And crowned for a day,
She walks to the altar of Artemis,
Where she will nod her noble head to the blade
And shower the sacred stones
With her bright blood
For a long, bloody harvest.

Child, your father is waiting
With a last libation,
To make you pure enough to die.
The army too waits on you,
But thinks only of Troy.

Hail, Artemis, daughter of Zeus,
Mistress of the gods,
We sing your praise
And pray for something bright
At the end of this darkness.
Mistress, Lady,
If indeed you have a taste for human blood,
Escort the armies of Greece
To Phrygian shores,
To the treacherous towers of Troy.
There may you one day
Crown the head of Agamemnon
And garland the spears of his men
With glorious victory.
Lady, we ask of you,
Let the story begun today
Live forever.

IPHIGENIA IN TAURIS

CHARACTERS

In Order of Appearance

Iphigenia
Daughter of Agamemnon, Priestess of the Temple of Artemis
    in the Land of the Taurians

Orestes
Brother of Iphigenia

Pylades
Orestes' Cousin and Companion, Husband to Elektra

Chorus
Captive Greek Women

Choral Leader
Leader of the Chorus

Herdsman
A Taurian

Attendants
To the Temple and the King

Thoas
King of the Taurians

Messenger
One of Thoas' Guards

Athena
Daughter of Zeus

The scene is the temple precinct of Artemis, on the Taurian coast. The steps of the temple lead to a blood-stained altar. Trophies of the dead lie about, propped against the temple walls.

Iphigenia enters from the inner sanctuary of the temple.

Agamemnon

I am Iphigenia,
    seed of Agamemnon, flower of Klytemnestra.
My house is the house of Atreus, son of Pelops,
    whose matchless steeds, gifts of Poseidon,
        won him his wife.
Two sons she bore to Atreus,
    Menelaos, my uncle, and Agamemnon,
    who took to his bed the daughter of Tyndareos,
        my mother.
I am Iphigenia,
    for Helen's sake a living sacrifice to Artemis,
    slain, for all my father knows, on the cliffs of Aulis,
    near the dark sea pools spun and whirled white
        in the straits of Euripos.
There in the bay of Aulis
    a thousand sails hung limp,
        the Greek armada,
    the fleet of Agamemnon, King of Kings,
        launched to seize the crown of victory
            and to avenge a spoiled bed.
All this to appease a cuckold's lost pride.
But it came to nothing there, in Aulis,
    where the winds grew still as stone,
        and ships leaned over in the sand.
A proud king resorted to a prouder priest.
Agamemnon bent and knelt and listened,
    while Kalkhas read the sacred flames:
"Lord Agamemnon, you lead this vast Greek force nowhere.
Never will your ships leave their beds of sand
    until you grant Artemis her due --
        your daughter, Iphigenia,
    as victim at my altar.

Your vow of long ago was clear --
        to yield to the goddess of light
                the year's first and loveliest fruit.
That vow is overdue.
The child born in your halls,
        lifted high by your wife
                and proclaimed loveliest of all
        is mine to stain my altars with her blood."

Odysseus spun the tale
        that plied me from my mother's arms.
She bathed me for my husband's bed,
        wove the wedding crown,
                and sang to me.
Bride of Akhilleus,
        ill-starred and marked for slaughter,
                I went to Aulis.
There I was seized and held by many hands.
Flames beneath and blade above,
        death closed in on me.
But goddess Artemis stole me from the knife and fire,
        leaving a deer to bleed and burn in my stead,
        while I was blown through the luminous aether
                here, to Taurica,
                a barbarous land with a barbarous king.
The king's name is Thoas, which means "swift,"
        a name he won with his feet.
Priestess of Artemis is my post here,
        hostess to her altars.
I please her with the rites I keep, prescribed by sacred law,
        festivals in name only.
Fear holds my tongue from saying more than this:
        I make a sacrifice of any hapless Greek
                who stumbles on these shores.
Such is the custom here, long before I came.
I raise no blade, except to cut the victim's hair.
I spill no blood, only water.
Inside, there, in her -- the divine one's -- inner rooms,
        other hands do the butchering.
I have no words for what they do.

Now, in hope of some release, I face the morning light
        and tell the dark visions come in night.
In sleep I saw myself in Argos.
My exile here was past.
I was sleeping, a virgin among virgins,
        and the earth beneath me quaked.
I fled to the open sky and saw my house fall, stone by stone.
One lone column stood when all else fell,
        the centerpost of my father's house.
This post, it seemed to me, grew golden locks,
        streaming from its capital and flowing down its sides.
It spoke with a human voice.
I paid to it my familiar rites.
As if it were another stranger marked for death,
I spattered it with holy water, bent and wept.

This I tell you, is the meaning of my dream:
        the victim I made ready, the one now dead,
                is Orestes.
For the pillars of a house are its sons.
And my rites mean sure death.
If I could read these phantoms in any other way, I would.
But I cannot.
Instead, I do all that is left me now to do.

Calling out.

Come, women, Greek women like myself,
        gifts of our barbarian king.
Come near and companion me.
I am far from my brother,
        and he is far from me.
I will lift this cup and pour it out
        in sweet memory of him.
Why do they not come?
I must go inside . . .

Turning and facing the temple.

        the temple of Artemis.
It is where I live.

She re-enters the temple.

Enter Orestes and Pylades.

Orestes

Look, a path!
See if anyone's coming.

Pylades

I'm looking . . . and I don't see anyone.

Orestes

There.

Pointing to the temple.

Pylades, do you think that's it --
        what we've sailed all the way from Argos to find --
            the shrine of Artemis?

Pylades

Yes, that must be it, Orestes.

Orestes

And is that the altar
        where they spill the blood of Greeks?

Pylades

See for yourself the dark stains down its sides.

Orestes

And there, stacked against the wall . . .
        the dead men's spoils.

Pylades

Trophies left by strangers
        long since stacked beneath the ground.
We had best be on our toes.

96

Orestes

O Phoibos,
      why do you lay another snare for me
        when I have done your word,
      avenged my father with my mother's blood?
Wave after wave of blood-eyed Furies
      have driven me from my home,
        hounded me down endless paths.
I came to you a suppliant, on my knees,
      asking no more than to see an end to my trials.
I begged release from the whirling wheel of madness
      that spun me throughout Greece like a lost star.
You told me to come here, to Taurica,
      to the altar of your sister Artemis,
        to seize her graven image,
      fallen, they say, from heaven to this very place.
Once I had braved every danger and --
      whether by my own wits or by witless luck --
      had laid my hands upon the holy likeness,
        I was to make of it a gift to Greece.
That was it.
Nothing more was asked of me.
Release from my woes was one last daring deed away.

So here I am, obedient to your words,
      in a land unmapped and unwelcoming.

Pylades, my companion, I need your advice.
What now?
You see the height of that wall.
How could we hope to scale it without being seen?
And we'd be taking quite a risk
      trying to force open those brazen doors,
        when we know nothing of their strength.
And we would be as good as dead, if we're caught up there,
      prying loose the hinges
        and scheming our way into the temple.
I suggest we cheat death,
      and go back where we came from.

Pylades
Run away? You can't be serious.
We've never run away from anything.
And it is no time to turn coward,
          when we are on god's business.
I suggest we quit the temple now
          and hide in the cliff-side caves
                    where the dark tides bathe the gleaming rocks.
We want to be far from our ship for now.
All it would take would be for one wandering eye
          to spot our mast and sound the alarm;
                    and they would be down on us like that.
Instead, we wait in the caves for obscuring night to fall.
And then we use whatever nerve and knack we have
          to make off with the temple's glorious relic.
Make note of those projecting beams,
          up there in the temple eaves.
There's space enough between them for the two of us
          to lower ourselves down.
It will be a challenge; but that's what brave men are for.
Cowards come to nothing anyway.
Besides, if all we plan to do is turn around,
          this was a long way to row.

Orestes
You speak well, the kind of words I can't ignore.
We best go and find our hiding-place.
Phoibos will not stand by and let his word be mocked.
So we must dare to do it.
The fact that it won't be easy is no excuse in youth.

Orestes and Pylades exit.

98

Chorus

Silence.
Let holy silence
Shroud this land of hostile seas and clashing rocks.
O goddess of the hunt,
Mountain-wild child of Leto,
We lift our pale feet in ritual steps
To approach your holy place
Roofed in gleaming gold.
Spotless we serve the spotless one,
The keeper of the key,
Locked away in exile here
From all that once brought joy
In the land of our fathers.

To Iphigenia.

What is it?
What draws your face so?
Child of the famed king
Whose scudding ships and bronze-helmed men
Swarmed against the towered walls of Troy
Like a plague of locusts,
Child, why have you summoned us here?

Iphigenia

Women, I am lost in my own laments.
Like an unstrung lyre, I make sounds, but never song.
Aiaiaiai.
This night has brought dark sights to me.
Banished from the day, they fester in my darkened heart.
I have seen my brother perished.
These tears are for him.
As for me, I am lost.
The last pillar of my father's house
Lies among the ruins.
We are extinct.
Argos, who will sing what you endured?
I curse whatever thieving power
        plunged my only brother into hell.

99

Sweet brother,
I take this bowl and mix the drink of the dead:
     warm milk of a mountain heifer,
     swirling wine sweet to Bakkhos,
     the flowing toil of tawny bees.
Down through a thirsty earth to hell
     I shall pour this gift to appease the dead
        and to charm their king.
To one of the women.
Give me the purple urn
     and the drink for the god of death.

Scion of Agamemnon, Brother, wherever you lie in darkness,
     these gifts are yours.
Take them from my hands.
I cannot come to your tomb,
     cut my hair and weep over you.
Not that I lie in some miserable grave,
     slaughtered, as men think, long ago.
I am in exile, far from our home.

Chorus
Lady, our chants echo your grief,
Wild laments,
Litanies learned from barbarians
For times of death and loss.
We sing the dirge of the dead,
Intoned by their king,
A song without a hint of hope.

100

Lament the house of Atreus.
Lament the house of your fathers.
The brilliant, blinding sceptre of Agamemnon
Is dark as blackest night.
Who is left of all the shining Argive kings
To mount the throne?
Wave after wave of havoc
Crashed against that house
Before it fell.
There was the charioteer,
Whose winged steeds circuited the sky,
Until Pelops toppled him,
As the sacred sun changed course
And turned askance.
The lamb with golden fleece
Brought its own train of horrors,
Each murder and grief
Spawning its successor.
The river of revenge for the slain sons of Tantalos
Crests and quits its banks.
And now the last of the line
Must know a force
Zealous for its ruin.

Iphigenia

My evil fate and I were conceived on the same night
            in the same bed.
We were born of the same womb
            and reared to full stature in the same house.
Klytemnestra, ill-starred child of Leto,
            wooed the plumed princes of Greece
                    before she lay back in Agamemnon's bed
            and misconceived me, her first fruit,
                        for unholy slaughter.
It was for my father's final shame that
I was born and suckled.
Drawn by snow-white mares, I came to sandy Aulis,
            bride of Akhilleus . . . mockery!
It was a match made in hell.

Now, I live a stern life.
Exiled to the shore of a hostile sea,
    I am unwed, barren, homeless,
        without the solace of a friend.
I have no songs for Argive Hera.
I weave no tales of Titans or Pallas Athena
    in vivid tapestries, on a deep-thrumming loom.
Instead I splash the blood of strangers over grim altars.
Their hideous groans and despairing tears inspire pity
    but not song.

Now my heart eludes their pain and feels its own.
I mourn my brother dead in Argos.
Orestes, I left you clinging to your mother's breast,
    a babe without blemish,
        with a blush in your cheeks.
You were the crown prince of Argos,
        and mother held you close.

Choral Leader

Look. A herdsman comes from the shore.
He seems to have something to tell us.

Herdsman

Child of Agamemnon and Klytemnestra, hear me.
I have strange news for you.

Iphigenia

There is panic in your voice. Why?

Herdsman

Two young men, with pluck and arms of steel,
        have rowed through the clashing rocks
            and landed on our shore.
They will make a suiting sacrifice,
        a gift to please the goddess.
Quickly, prepare your rites.
Fetch your basin and draw the lustral waters.

Iphigenia

These strangers, where do they come from?
Could you tell from their look?

Herdsman

They're Greeks, that much I know.
It's hard to say beyond that.

Iphigenia

You didn't hear either of their names?

Herdsman

I heard the one fellow call the other one "Pylades."

Iphigenia

And this Pylades' companion, what of his name?

Herdsman

I can't say. We heard nothing more.

Iphigenia

How did you happen to come upon them?
Tell me how you took them.

Herdsman

Well, we were down at the sea's edge . . . in the breakers . . .
   not far from the perilous strait.

Iphigenia

Interrupting.

Herdsmen? . . . in the sea?

Herdsman

We went there to wash our cattle in the brine.
It's something we do.

Iphigenia

O . . . well . . . then let's go back.
Tell me, how did you capture them?
This I want to know.
They have surely taken their time in getting here.
Long has the altar of the goddess
        thirsted for Greek blood.

Herdsman

As I was telling you,
        we had driven our cattle down to the sea,
                near where the churning currents
      thread the clashing rocks.
There is a cliff-side cave down there,
        a favorite fishers' haunt,
           carved from the sheer rock face by a determined sea.
That was where one of our company caught sight of the pair,
        and tiptoed back to tell us.
His heart leapt to his mouth as he spoke:
        "Look. Don't you see them? Sitting . . . there . . .
        gods for sure . . . of some sort!"
At the sight of the two, another of us, a god-fearing man,
        lifted his hands in prayer:
      "Lord Palamon, guardian of ships," he chanted,
      "child of Leukothea, goddess of the seas, be gracious.
      Be gracious, too, yonder gods, whoever you are,
        perhaps the holy twins of Zeus,
                or else two favorites of Nereus,
                father of the fifty ocean-nymphs."
But another one of us, a rude and reckless fellow,
        was quick to mock this cant.
"Shipwrecked sailors," he taunted,
        "no more, no less . . .
      cowering among the hollow rocks
      because they know how we welcome strangers here."

These words made sense to almost everyone.
And the two became our quarry,
        victims to be hunted for this altar's rites.

Meanwhile, one of the strangers left the cave
        and stood on a cleft of jagged rock.
His head flew about, up and down, as if on a string.
His hands and arms shook with frenzy
        and he gave out ungodly groans.
Then, with the voice of a hunter on the leash,
        hurled along by dogs who've caught the scent,
            he cried out:
        "Pylades, don't you see them? . . . There! . . . There!
        Hellish fiends, craving my death.
            knotted snakes for hair . . .
        They lick and tear at me . . . with fangs of fire . . .
            There!
        Winged scorching demon . . . sheets of flame!
            Her breath burns my soul.
        In her arms . . .   Mother!
        She holds you like a giant rock . . . to hurl . . .
                splinter me . . .
            like a pestle to grind me into . . .
        Where? Where can I flee?"

None of this, nothing of what he said
        was there to be seen by us.
There were cattle and dogs nearby.
And it must have been their lowing and barks
        that he took for the screams of furies.
We drew together and sat close, in silence,
        as if we were the ones whose lives hung by a thread.
But then he drew his sword and leapt among our cattle,
        like a hungry lion.
He thrusted and hacked at the sorry beasts,
            as if to beat back his assailing demons,
        until the curling sea beneath his feet
            bubbled and foamed red with their blood.
This was more than we could sit and watch.
We stood and blew our blaring conch-horns
        to sound the alarm
    and swell our ranks with any who would come.
As we herdsmen stood, we counted ourselves no match
        for bold and brawny foreigners half our age.

But soon we had the numbers that we needed,
        just as the stranger's madness left him.
Drool spewed down his face and beard,
        as his legs wobbled and refused his weight.
One down. It was our chance.
In one barrage after another, we pelted them with rocks,
        hurled with all our might.
The one man did all that lay within him
        to shield his fallen friend.
He wiped the spittle from his chin
        and made a wall of his heavy cloak,
                dodging or warding off our hailing blows
                        as best he could.
Then the stricken one regained his wits and sprang to his feet.
He groaned when he saw the battle's tide coming in
        and marked the ruin it carried in its wake.
We closed in, throwing all the harder.
And that same one let out one last cry,
                defiant and despairing:
                "Pylades, we are going to our death. Let's do it right.
                Draw your sword and follow me!"
At the sight of those two brandishing their swords . . .
                well, we ran . . . to the nearby woods . . .
        and tried to look like trees.
Not all at once . . .   Some threw stones while others ran.
And when these were routed,
        the others gathered stones and took their place.
The wonder is that with the sky all but darkened
                with flying rocks, not one struck its mark.

The fact is we took them in the end
                without any daring on our part.
We kept circling them and throwing our rocks,
        until we knocked the swords from their hands
                        and they collapsed in sheer exhaustion.

We marched them to the king;
        and he, after one look, sends them to you,
                for the sprinkling of the holy waters
        and the letting of their foreign blood.

Maiden, you used to pray that victims such as these
        might come along.
For when you slaughter them and their kind,
        Hellas begins to pay the price
                for what it would have done to you in Aulis.
Your blood they almost shed cries out for theirs.

Choral Leader

There is something wondrous to your tale
        about this stranger Greek -- whoever he is --
            come across the hostile sea.

Iphigenia

To the Herdsman.

Well, then, go and fetch these strangers.
And I will see that all is ready for them.

The Herdsman exits.

Iphigenia

Wretched heart within me,
You used to be so gentle toward strangers.
Always you showed such pity.
And, when Greeks fell into your hands,
        you wept familial tears.
Now it is all different.
These dread dreams of Orestes dead untame my heart
        and set it wild.
New guests here will find me severe, like slate.
Friends, now I know how true it is that,
              when life turns harsh,
        the heart grows hard, not soft.

Through the twin-rock portals of this land,
               never yet has any god-sent wind or ship
        brought me Helen, my undoing, nor Menelaos.
To them . . . I have a debt to pay,
        in memory of Aulis.

107

There, like some bellowing heifer,
I was seized by the Greek chiefs.
My father -- my own father -- played hierophant.
He would have slain me.
It is a nightmare ten thousand dawns cannot erase.
How I twined myself around my father's knees
                and groped upwards to touch his beard.
I remember my very words:
        "Father, this match you make for me is mockery!
                Imagine it as it will be:
        Mother and the Argive women full with song . . .
        Festive flutes fill the air . . .
        You lead me to the altar . . .
                        and give me away . . . with a knife.
        You marry me to Hades, not the son of Peleus.
        With sheer deceit you coaxed me to a bloody bed."
When I left my home in Argos,
        I hid and blushed behind my wedding veil.
I was too shy to take my brother, now dead, into my arms
                or to give my sister a good-bye kiss.
Farewells were overlooked.
There would be time for them when I returned.
Mine were a bride's thoughts . . . of Akhilleus . . .
                and of his bed.

O wretched Orestes, if you are really dead,
        how cheated you are of so much
                that might have been.
Father had such plans for you!

Turning toward the shrine.

Goddess,
        your subtleties elude me.
We mortals are unclean, unworthy of approaching you,
        if we soil our hands with bloodshed,
                touch a corpse
                        or assist a woman giving birth.
And yet you yourself revel in human sacrifice.
You find it sweet.
No, this cannot be!

108

Zeus and Leto his bride
    cannot have spawned
        anything so spurious.
I don't believe the tale of Tantalos
    and his feast.
I don't believe that gods ever savored
    the flesh of a child.
Here, in this land, men, not gods, are murderers.
Men make their own perversions into rituals
        and sacralize their sins.
No god is evil.
That is what I believe.

Chorus
Dark twin cliffs
Where two seas meet,
And continents converge,
Where Io in her agony,
Driven out of Argos,
Crossed over in flight
From Europe to Asian soil,
Who are these strangers?
Have they come from the fair waters of Eurotas,
Woven thick with reeds?
Or the sweet stream of Dirke?
Who are they come to this savage land
Where the altars of the child of Zeus
And the pillars of her shrine
Are splashed with human blood?

Was it simple greed for gold
That urged these men to hoist their sails
And ride the heaving waves?
Did their heavy fir-wood oars
Plow the angry sea
In quest of foreign spoils?
This dream of distant sparkling plunder
Is sweet beyond the toll of grief it takes.
Insatiate addicts they will become
Who roam the remotest seas
And prowl cities unknown,
Lured beyond the reach of their wits.
Their lust is all they share.
This one strikes it rich,
While that one's luck
Runs out.

How did they thread the clashing rocks
And skirt the sleepless beaches
Of harpy-haunted Phineus,
Scudding across the breakers
To the far beach of Amphitrite,
Where the chorus of fifty sea-nymphs
Weave a circle with their steps,
Chanting and dancing
To the rhythms of the sea?
How did they sail so far across the hostile sea,
As the winds tore at the sails
And the rudder groaned,
To Leuke where the sea-birds flock
And where Akhilleus once
Raced the glistening strand?

If only our mistress' prayers
Might come true,
And Helen, Leda's darling,
Quitting Troy's splendid walls,
Come here,
To have her legendary locks
Splashed with sacrificial waters
Just before our mistress
Slits her soft pale throat
And collects an old debt.
But the sweetest news of all would be
If some Greek seafarer would come to bring an end
To our exile and our bondage.
Our dreams are of home,
To see the walls and the towers of our city,
And to sing with one and all the festal songs.

Temple Attendants enter with Orestes and Pylades.

Choral Leader

See, here they come,
        the two we've heard so much about, tightly trussed,
                the latest catch, fresh for slaughter.
Silence, friends, let us admire the pride of Greece,
        washed up on our shore,
                true to all the herdsman told us.

Goddess, accept this sacrifice,
        if this land's ways suit you.
But in Greece
        our laws give another name
                        to what's done here.

Enter Iphigenia.

Iphigenia

Let us proceed.
Scrupulously, I must see that all is done
        as the goddess prescribes.

111

Untie the strangers' hands.
They are hallowed now, and not to be bound.
Go within the temple.
Make all things ready.
And in doing so,
          overlook no observance,
          heed every canon.

*Chorus and Attendants exit into the temple, leaving Iphigenia
alone with Orestes and Pylades.*

Iphigenia

Moaning.

Your mother . . . your father . . . who are they?
Tell me if you have a sister . . . and her name.
Her heart will break to lose the two of you.
There is no charting the path of fate.
No one knows who will suffer next, or why.
The gods cast our lots behind our backs.
Fate makes no sound until it catches up with us . . .
          as it has with you.
Tell me, where have you come from?
It seems to me you have come a long way, only to go down
          below . . . without hope.

Orestes

Woman, whoever you are, why all these dark words
          and deep moans?
You are only adding weight to a heavy burden.
Anyone facing death who thinks that tears will bring
          reprieve, I call a fool.
If there is salvation at the gates of hell,
          it doesn't come from groaning.
You double what we endure,
          when you add folly to our fate.
Let these things take their course.
Spare us your pity.
We already know what goes on in there.
You have no news to break slowly to us.

112

Iphigenia

But there is something I want to learn from you.
Which of you is called "Pylades"?

Orestes

He is. Now aren't you glad you know that!

Iphigenia

From what Greek city?

Orestes

Woman, what difference could it make?

Iphigenia

Are you half-brothers . . . or do you have the same mother?

Orestes

Neither.
Our love makes us one.

Iphigenia

To Orestes.

And you, what did your father call you?

Orestes

My name should be "Accursed."

Iphigenia

That wasn't what I asked.
I know the name that Fate has given you.

Orestes

If I die without a name,
            no one will know how to mock me when I'm gone.

Iphigenia

Are you so proud as to begrudge me this?

Orestes

You may carve up my body. Yes, my name I begrudge you.

Iphigenia

Then tell me this much . . . the name of your city.

Orestes

Give up . . . as I have. I'm as good as dead.

Iphigenia

Think of it as a favor. Please, why not?

Orestes

Argos . . . glorious Argos. I say it proudly.

Iphigenia

Stranger, this is the truth? You swear it.
Argos is your home?

Orestes

I was born in Mykene, when it was flourishing.

Iphigenia

Why did you leave? Were you exiled?

Orestes

You might call it exile, except that I left on my own
    as much as I was driven out.

Iphigenia

I'm so glad you've come.
I've longed for someone from Argos.

114

Orestes

Then this is your lucky day . . . not mine.

Iphigenia

One more question . . . Can I ask you one more thing?

Orestes

I suppose it can't make things much worse.

Iphigenia

Famed Troy . . . do you know of it?

Orestes

I wish I didn't . . . not even as a bad dream.

Iphigenia

They say it is gone, carried off on the tips of Greek spears.

Orestes

You heard right.
Troy is no more.

Iphigenia

And Helen . . . did Menelaos take her home?

Orestes

She came home . . . doing no good to my house.

Iphigenia

She owes me as well.
Where is she now?

Orestes

Sparta . . . in her old bed.

Iphigenia

Bitch! I hate her . . . and so must all of Greece.

Orestes

Including me.
Her switching beds did me no good.

Iphigenia

And the Greek fleet . . . are the rumors true?
Are they home?

Orestes

You expect a "yes" or "no" to that?
I can't tell you everything in one word.

Iphigenia

Then tell me all there is to tell . . . now, before you die.

Orestes

If that is what you wish, question me
and I will tell you what I know.

Iphigenia

The priest, Kalkhas . . . did he return?

Orestes

From what I heard he perished.

Iphigenia

Good. Well done, Artemis!
And Odysseus?

Orestes

They say he is alive . . . but not yet home.

116

Iphigenia

May he never get there.

Orestes

I think he's doing badly enough on his own,
        without your curses.

Iphigenia

And the child of Nereid Thetis . . . Akhilleus?
Does he live?

Orestes

No. In Aulis his wedding came to nothing.

Iphigenia

As those who endured it know too well.
Treachery, nothing more!

Orestes

For someone with no answers,
        you know the questions all too well.
Who are you, anyway?

Iphigenia

I too am from Greece, though I died to her long ago,
        when I was a child.

Orestes

Now it makes sense why you long so for any news of her.

Iphigenia

What of her general, the man they call the "blessed king"?

Orestes

I know of no blessed kings. Whom do you have in mind?

117

Iphigenia

King Agamemnon, son of Atreus.

Orestes

I know nothing. Woman . . . stop. No more!

Iphigenia

Friend, I beg you. Not until you've answered me,
    and brought me gladness.

Orestes

The king you think blessed is not.
He is dead . . . and his death has ruined another.

Iphigenia

Reeling and groaning with pain.

Dead? How? No!

Orestes

Why are you so upset?
What was he to you?

Iphigenia

The death of such splendor . . . it is upsetting.

Orestes

Even more upsetting is how his own wife slew him . . .
    with an axe.

Iphigenia

I weep for them both.

Orestes

No . . . no more.
We end here.

Iphigenia

No, we cannot. I must know more.
Does she live?

Orestes

No more.
Her son -- the one she gave life -- took hers.

Iphigenia

A house gone mad! Why did he do it?

Orestes

To avenge his father's death.

Iphigenia

How well he crossed perversity with justice.

Orestes

Not so well does he fare with the gods,
        regardless of his justice.

Iphigenia

Then who remains?
Which of Agamemnon's offspring is left at home?

Orestes

One daughter, Elektra, not yet come of age.

Iphigenia

The other daughter, the one they sacrificed . . .
        what is said of her?

Orestes

What is there to say?
She's dead and gone to darkness.

119

Iphigenia

She and her murderous father . . .
    both cursed in what he did.

Orestes

A shameless deed . . . for a shameless woman's sake.

Iphigenia

The boy, the dead king's son . . . does he live?
In Argos still?

Orestes

He lives a wretched life . . . nowhere and everywhere.

Iphigenia

False dreams, I am rid of you.
You meant nothing in the end.

Orestes

Even the so-called wisdom of the gods
        tells fewer lies
                than do our fleeting dreams.
It is difficult to overestimate the prevailing chaos
        among things human and divine.

But the one real human tragedy
        is when we set aside our common sense
            and put our faith in oracles
                    only to be ruined by them.
I know the truth of this firsthand,
        which is the way the truth is learned.

Choral Leader

And what of us . . . and the parents who bore us?
They may live. They may not.
We will never know.

120

Iphigenia

Listen closely, strangers.
I think I have a scheme to suit us both.
Surely there is no reason to complain
            when the same hammer pounds two nails.
Now this is what I propose.

To Orestes.

Your life I will spare, provided that you go to Argos,
            and take a message to my family there.
I have a letter, written by a man who pitied me.
He was a victim here, who saw my hands too were tied.
He grasped what simply is the case here,
            that murder is the rule of law for a goddess
                    who sees sacrifice as her just desserts.
I have had this letter for some time
            but no one to take it back to Argos.
You are a free man, if you will be the one
            to place it in the hands of someone dear to me.
If you are the man you say you are,
            nobly born and no stranger to Mykene,
            likely even to know the one to whom I send you,
                    and if I am right you bear me no ill will,
                            then save yourself.
It is not a bad swap, your life for a letter.
But as for him, my hands are tied.
You will go your way, and he his . . . to death,
            in there . . . on an altar.

Orestes

Strange woman, your words are music to my ears,
            except for one wrong note.
I don't take lightly your slaughtering my friend.
I steered the ship that brought him here.
He came along on my behalf,
            to lend his shoulder to my burdens.
It would seem a strange form of justice now,
            for me to buy your favor and my freedom
                    with his life.

121

I have a counterplan.
Give him the letter. Send him to Argos.
It would be all the same to you.
Let me be the one to stay behind
        and feed the sacrificial flames.
It is a sad and shameful day
        when, in dark times,
                a man tosses away friendship
                        like a bad idea,
                and sells out his friend to save himself.

Iphigenia

You are a pure spirit, free of dross.
You must be well-born to give such loyalty to your friends.
How I pray that the one man left in my family
        might resemble you.
For I have a brother, though he is never before my eyes.
Yes, you may have your way.
Your friend will run my errand and you will die.
I wonder at your zeal on his behalf
        and not on your own.

Orestes

Whose dread calling is it to preside over my sacrifice?

Iphigenia

Mine. It is my office to supplicate the goddess.

Orestes

You are a girl with not a very enviable occupation.
I find you most unfortunate.

Iphigenia

I do what I must do.

Orestes

Does that include wielding the sacrificial knife?

Iphigenia

No. I will sprinkle harmless water on your hair.

Orestes

I don't mean to pry.
But if not you, then who is the local butcher?

Iphigenia

They are inside.

Orestes

Once I'm dead, where will I lie?

Iphigenia

Inside, among the sacred flames . . .
        then scattered into a crevasse.

Orestes

If only my sister might be here to see to my rites.

Iphigenia

Whoever you are, you are cursed,
        and your prayers must fall on deaf ears.
You can see as well as I how far your sister is
        from these uncivilized shores.
But since you and I chance to share in Argos
        a common home,
                I will do all I can to attend to you.
I will strew your bier with bright gifts
        and with golden oil.
I will moisten your remains.
Over the loud licking flames of your pyre
        I will pour sweet lucent honey,
                the proud work of wild mountain bees.

But now I must go inside and fetch the letter.
Please try to think well of me.

123

To the Guards.

Guards, watch them. But otherwise let them be.

To herself.

Now I will send to Argos, to the one so dear to me,
      words beyond his hopes.
The one he thinks is dead is not.
I live and the news of me will be a sweet rain.

Iphigenia exits.

Choral Leader

To Orestes.

We pity you, marked for the sprinkling of lustral waters
      and for the dark-spattering spray of blood.

Orestes

Women, I am not to be pitied.
Farewell is enough said.

Choral Leader

To Pylades.

You are the lucky one.
You are the one blessed to see your home again.

Pylades

Am I to be envied when I lose my friend?

Choral Leader

To Pylades.

True enough, you run a grim errand.
Your life too is spoiled here.
When I ask myself which of you to mourn more,
      you who must perish, or you who must survive,
            my heart wavers and spins in confusion
            like a weathercock in a winter's storm.

124

Orestes

Pylades, are you thinking what I'm thinking?

Pylades

How can I know without your saying more?

Orestes

I'm thinking and wondering about our young priestess here.
Who can she be?
She knew enough and cared enough
      to ask about the trials we knew in Troy,
           the homecoming of the Greek fleet,
           and the fate of Kalkhas, skilled in augury.
She seemed so Greek when she spoke of Akhilleus
      and grieved to learn from me the unspeakable ends
          of wretched Agamemnon, his wife,
            and their cursed children.
She must indeed be from Argos.
For why else would she have launched
      such a wave of questions
         into the state and fate of Argos,
    as if they were her own?
And why would she be sending this letter of hers to Argos,
         unless Argos were her home?

Pylades

Your thoughts run ahead of mine.
I guess I would have said everything you've said
      except for one thing.
The calamities of kings are not secrets.
That she or anyone knows of them comes as no surprise.
It was something else she said that concerned me.

Orestes

What?
Share your concern,
    and we might resolve it together.

Pylades

For me to live on in the light, when you go down to darkness,
    shames me.
We have been companions for this much of the journey,
    and we must be companions the rest of the way . . .
    to death.
Otherwise, anywhere I go, in Argos,
    or across the countless valleys of Phokis,
        I will be called a coward and a snake.
You know what people are like,
    and you know what they will say:
        that I saved myself and made for home,
        leaving you without a second thought,
    or worse, that I took advantage
            of your family's disarray
    and took your life myself.
You must admit, the pieces of such a scheme lie at hand:
    your demise, your sister's hand,
        and a crown without a head to wear it.
You see what I fear and why I feel shame.
There can be no other way.
Together we must seize our last breaths,
    together slaughtered, together set ablaze.
I am your friend.
I will give no one the pretext
    for saying I was not.

Orestes

I wish you would say what makes some sense.
Count the fate at hand.
It is one, not two, and it is mine to bear.
And this painful reproach you speak of . . .
    will it not come down on me
        if I now take your life,
    you who cast your lot with me?

Consider my condition.
How bad can it be to let go of a life
    so plagued by the gods?

126

With you it is different. You are flourishing.
My house has fallen, crushed by an impious curse.
Your house stands firm, free of offense.
If you save yourself now,
          and give my sister -- your wife -- sons,
                    don't you see, you will let my name live?
Otherwise, my house and the house of my fathers,
          will be childless . . . blotted out . . . no more.
Go your way, not mine.
Live in my father's house.
I ask only this . . . give me your hand as a pledge . . .

Joining hands with Pylades.

          . . . that when you come to Greece again
          and to the plains of horse-breeding Argos,
                    you will heap up a burial mound
                              and mark it in memory of me.
There my sister will bend over me in painful grief
          and weep and cut her flowing hair.
Tell the story of how I perished,
          at the hands of some Argive woman,
                    flattened on an altar and offered up to death.
Never abandon my sister,
          no matter how desolate and despoiled
                    you find my father's house.

Goodbye, sweet friend. There has been no one like you.
Companions, we came of age together, fellows in the hunt,
          inseparable even in the darkest of times.

As for me, I was deceived and set upon a false course
          by Phoibos, the "prophet,"
                    who should have known better.
He plied his arts and drove me far from Greece,
          to the edges of the earth,
                    compliant with his shocking prophecies.
To his words, I gave my total trust.
I've held nothing back,
          taking my mother's life
          and losing my own.

Pylades

Friend so cursed, you shall have your tomb,
      and never will I betray your sister's bed.
In death you shall know from me
      a loyalty beyond any you've known in life.
But you are not yet in death,
      no matter how near the edge you stand.
And, until you are, the oracle is not confuted.
When the wheel of fate turns,
      there is no night so black
          that it cannot yield the dawn.

Orestes

No more.
It is too late for Phoibos and his fancy words.
See, she comes for me.

Iphigenia enters, holding the letter in her hand.

Iphigenia

To the guards, who exit at her command.

Go and lend a hand inside to those preparing for the sacrifice.

To Orestes and Pylades.

Friends, here it is, my letter, many pages long.
But I am still not at ease with our plans;
      so hear me out.
A man with a noose around his neck
      is not the same without his noose.
He moves all too soon from trembling fear
      to boldness and complacency.

To Pylades.

In short, once you've quit this place,
      I fear how soon you will forget your mission to Argos
        and deliver this letter, instead,
          to the nearest wave.

128

Orestes

What more do you want?
What would you need to put your fears to rest?

Iphigenia

An oath. Let him swear that he will take this letter to Argos
        and himself place it in the hands
                of him whom I shall name.

Orestes

And what corresponding pledge
        are you prepared to offer him?

Iphigenia

Tell me what you have in mind.
What do you want done or not done?

Orestes

I want him to leave this barbarous land alive.

Iphigenia

So do I. How else could he carry my letter?

Orestes

But will the king consent to this?

Iphigenia

I will persuade the king and myself see your friend off to sea.

Orestes

To Pylades.

Swear as she asks.

To Iphigenia.

Go ahead, formulate a fitting oath.

129

Iphigenia

To Pylades.

Swear that you will give this letter to my family.

Pylades

I swear that I will give that letter to your family.

Iphigenia

And I, for my part, swear that I will see you safely
    through the clashing rocks.

Orestes

To what god or goddess do you swear this?

Iphigenia

To Artemis . . .
    whose temple I attend to.

Pylades

And I to Zeus . . .
    august lord of heaven.

Iphigenia

And if you violate your oath and do me wrong?

Pylades

Then may I never know a homecoming.
And what of you, if you fail to rescue me?

Iphigenia

May I too never again set foot alive in Argos.

Pylades

But there is something that our oaths have overlooked.

Iphigenia

It is not too late to include your new concern,
> if it is fair.

Pylades

I ask one exception to what I've sworn.
If my ship is somehow wrecked at sea,
> and your letter with all else sinks beneath the waves,
> so that I've saved nothing but my very life,
>> I ask my oath be null and void.

Iphigenia

Don't you know that, with a precaution or two,
> most disasters can be averted?
I will simply tell you now the contents
> of the letter you are to deliver.
Then the message will be safe in any event.
If my letter arrives intact,
> in silence it will tell my tale.
But if it sinks into the sea, you will save my words
> as you save your very life.

Pylades

What you've said addresses my concerns as well as yours.
So tell me the core of your message
> and who it is in Argos to whom it must be brought.

Iphigenia

Go to Orestes, son of Agamemnon,
> and tell him this: "Your sister, the victim of Aulis,
>> though dead to Argos, lives
>> and sends you greetings, Iphigenia . . .

Orestes

Where . . . where is she?
Has she risen from the dead?

131

Iphigenia

I am she . . . the one you see now with your own eyes.
But don't interrupt.
Now where was I?
"Dear brother, come and take me back to Argos,
        before I die.
Set me free from this barbarous land . . .
        and from the sacrificial rites
            in which it is my sacred office to preside
        over the slaughtering of strangers . . . "

Orestes

Pylades, what can I say?
Are we dreaming this?

Iphigenia

" . . . or else I will be a curse upon your house, Orestes."

To Pylades,

Twice now you've heard that name,
        so don't forget it.

Orestes

O gods.

Iphigenia

Are you praying?
Why should you?
These are my affairs.

Orestes

Never mind. Continue.
I was thinking of something else.

Aside.

But I will come back soon enough to these marvels
        with a question of my own.

Iphigenia

Tell him: "It was Artemis who saved me,
        substituting the fawn my father sacrificed.
        For all my father knew,
            my breast received his sharpened blade.
        It was the goddess too who brought me here."
In sum this is what the letter says.

Pylades

Woman, the promises you have made to me
        appear all the more gracious now, when I see
        how easy it will be to keep my pledge to you.
In fact, why should I wait another moment
        to make good my word to you?
Look.

To Orestes.

Orestes, I bring and place in your hand
        this letter from your sister.

Pylades gives the letter to Orestes.

Orestes

Taking it.

And I receive it from your hand.
I let my fingers taste the pages.
They are sweet even before I read them.

To Iphigenia.

My beloved sister, hearing what I've heard,
        my wits leave me and my mind fades.
Even my arms doubt you.   Come . . .

Approaching Iphigenia.

I want to hold you,
        so that my invalid soul might dance again.

Orestes embraces Iphigenia.

Iphigenia

Pulling away.

Stranger, you sin!
I am the virgin priestess of Artemis.
I belong to her.
Your arms . . . your touch . . . defile me!

Orestes

Sister, child of Agamemnon, your father and mine,
      don't turn away now,
            not when you have me, your brother,
                  the one you stopped hoping for.

Iphigenia

I have . . . you . . . my brother?
Won't you stop?
My brother is in Argos . . . in Nauplia.

Orestes

Poor unfortunate, that is not where your brother is.

Iphigenia

Who bore you?
Was it the Spartan daughter of Tyndareos?

Orestes

Yes. To the grandson of Pelops.
I am his seed.

Iphigenia

What are you saying?
Can you prove any of this?

Orestes

All of it.
Ask me questions about our father's house.

Iphigenia

Just go on talking.
By listening I will learn what I need to know.

Orestes

First . . . something Elektra told me.
You know about the feud that flamed
        between Atreus and Thyestes?

Iphigenia

Yes. I heard that it began over a golden lamb.

Orestes

Do you remember weaving that tale upon your loom?

Iphigenia

O dearest one,
        you are very close to opening wide my heart.

Orestes

This too on your loom: the sun turned back.

Iphigenia

It made a lovely tapestry.

Orestes

For your wedding in Aulis,
        your mother drew the lustral water.

Iphigenia

Yes. I remember well.
There was no marriage bliss to cloud my memories.

Orestes

And did you cut your hair and give it to your mother?

Iphigenia

I did . . . as a burial-token, in place of my body.

Orestes

You asked for proof.
Here is what my own eyes have seen.
In my father's house, I saw the ancient spear of Pelops,
      the one he used to kill Oinomaos at Pisa
          and win the virgin Hippodameia.
This spear lay hidden deep within the palace, in your room.

Iphigenia

*Giving way at last, she leaps into Orestes' arms and climbs
him like a tree.*

Dearest brother, it is you . . . no one else. It is you!
Sweet, sweet Orestes, I have you now,
      far from Argos and our home.
I hold you, my dearest treasure.

Orestes

And I hold you, my sister whom the world thought dead.
These tears I weep . . . how welcome, like a summer rain.
They fill your eyes too . . . not tears at all.
Beneath the grief I've known so long,
      my heart begins to leap.

Iphigenia

You were still so tiny when I left you.
Such a little one you were when I left home,
      such a darling little one,
          cradled in your nurse's arms.
My dried-up soul drinks you like the sweetest wine.
O, I am so happy.
There are no words for this.
What can I say?
What has come to us today . . .
      is too big for words.

Orestes

Together . . . as we are now . . . never again apart,
     may we find blessing.

Iphigenia

Friends, women at my side,
     it feels strange to know such joy.
I am almost afraid to move,
     for fear it will flit away,
          like a phantom or a butterfly.
I call out to our homeland, dear Mykene.
I call out to our hearth, the work of mighty Kyklops.
I give thanks for my brother's life, for his nurture . . .
     thanks that my brother was reared so tall and shining,
          to be the light of our house.

Orestes

Sister, we could not have been more blessed in our birth.
But then our fortunes fell from grace
     and blazed us a trail of grief.

Iphigenia

Cursed as I am, I know the truth of what you say.
How can I forget the gleaming blade
     my own wretched father lifted . . .

Orestes

O god, I can see it, even though I wasn't there.

Iphigenia

. . . near my throat?
Unwed and innocent, I fell into their trap,
     lured by the promise of Akhilleus' bed.
It was a bed of graven stone instead,
     drenched with tears and lustral waters,
          yet thirsting for the first flow of my virgin blood.
Even now I hear the wailing, my wedding song gone wrong.

137

Orestes

I too wail,
      when I think of what our cursed father dared to do.

Iphigenia

My lot assigned to me a father who unlearned his fatherhood.
It was a deadly curse, destined to repeat itself.

Orestes

Yes, by you and me . . . on the goddess' grim altar there,
      where a sister came all to close to . . .

Iphigenia

A heinous crime!
Dearest brother, it was unthinkable what I dared to do.
Unthinkable!
How narrow was your escape from these hands, my hands,
      which would have thrown you into hell.
But now, where does all this lead?
What fate now directs my course?
What door can I still open for you in this city of death?
How can I send you back to Argos now,
      before the sharpened blade spills your blood?
God-forsaken soul of mine,
      it is yours to find a way.
By land and not by ship?
Your feet, no matter how swift,
      will only run you to your death.
Barbarous tribes haunt every path
      and the roads in this land go nowhere.
Then by ship?
The seascape, through the clashing rocks,
      is a long way from here.
Lost . . . lost . . . I see no way.
What mortal cunning, divine power, or simple miracle
      will now accomplish our escape?
Who will save the last remaining hope
      of the house of Atreus?

138

Choral Leader

We have seen ourselves, not heard from others,
   this astonishing reunion.
Any telling of this tale must fall short of how it was.

Pylades

Orestes, nothing is more natural
   than to embrace a long-lost love.
But it is also time to wipe our tears and look at where we are.
If we think our safety is something worth the effort,
   we should be looking for a way out of here.
Anyone with any sense knows that whatever chance we have
   won't wait around for us.
I think the joys of this moment can be stretched out later.

Orestes

Well said and well taken.
But this time I feel that fate is working with us.
Even so, you are right.
The gods grow stronger on our behalf,
   when we lend a hand.

Iphigenia

But first one more question,
   no matter what the present urgency.
Please do not deny me this.
I must know my sister's lot in life.
Any news of her is precious to me.

Orestes

Married to this man,

Pointing to Pylades.

   her life is blessed.

Iphigenia

And this man . . . where is he from? Who is his father?

Orestes

His father's name is Strophios . . . of Phokis.

Iphigenia

I see . . . Atreus' daughter's son.
That makes us kin.

Orestes

Pylades is your cousin and my one true friend.

Iphigenia

Was he not yet born when father tried to kill me?

Orestes

Not yet.
Strophios was childless for quite some time.

Iphigenia

To Pylades.

Welcome, my sister's husband.

Orestes

To me he has been a savior, as well as kinsman.

Iphigenia

Orestes, tell me.
How did you dare do it?
How could you kill our mother?

Orestes

Please . . . shh . . . not that, Iphigenia . . .
            to avenge father . . . that is enough.

Iphigenia

But why would she have killed her husband?

Orestes

Let mother rest.
It doesn't make a pretty story.

Iphigenia

All right . . . but tell me, does Argos now await you?

Orestes

No. I am in exile. Menelaos rules.

Iphigenia

Our uncle . . . he affronts our stricken house?
He exiled you?

Orestes

No, not he. The dreadful furies drove me out of Argos.

Iphigenia

Was that the seizure they described, along the shore?

Orestes

Yes . . . not the first time I've provided
      such a wretched spectacle.

Iphigenia

I understand. They haunt you in mother's name.

Orestes

They force a bloody bit between my teeth.

Iphigenia

But what brought you here?

Orestes

The oracle. Phoibos commanded me to come.

141

Iphigenia

To do what?
Are you free to tell me?

Orestes

I will tell you all there is to tell.
First, the root of all my woes.
As soon as my hands avenged our mother's sin --
        the sin we left in silence --
        the furies harassed and hounded me into exile.
It was Loxias who guided my steps to Athens
        where I might appease those nameless fiends.
For in Athens there is a sacred court of law,
        established by Zeus
        to wash the blood-stained hands of Ares.
So I went there.

But so abhorrent to the gods was I
        that no one reached a hand to me.
I was without welcome.
Then some few pitied me
        and set for me a separate place.
I ate my meal under their roof,
        but not at their table.
They raised a wall of silence round me;
        so I ate and drank alone,
While they lifted their brimming cups
        and enjoyed themselves.
I had no harsh words for my hosts.
In silence I endured their slights
        as if I failed to notice them at all.
I moaned, instead, in grief over my mother,
        and what I had done to her.

Then I went to trial atop the mound of Ares.
Platformed on a slab of stone I stood and faced
        the eldest of the furies, stationed on a matching stone.
I answered the grim charges filed against me,
        indicting me with my mother's blood.

142

It was Phoibos who won my case for me.
His testimony saved me.
Pallas gave the tally of the votes, a verdict split in two,
        good enough for me to win the day
        and leave unscathed.
Those furies who consented to the court's decree
        set up a sacred residence nearby,
        while the rest resumed their tireless tormenting of me,
        in complete contempt of law.

And so it went until I came again to Apollo's holy ground.
I threw myself down before his sanctuary.
Flattened in the dust and fasting from all food,
        I vowed to cut all ties with life
        and expire on Phoibos' very steps
    unless he would undo what he had done to me
        and save me from his own destroying hand.

Then he spoke down to me,
        Phoibos from his golden tripod.
Here, to this place, he missioned me
        to seize the graven sky-dropped goddess
        and establish it on Attic soil.

Sister, be my accomplice now in winning that deliverance
        the god defined for me.
If we can but seize the holy likeness from the shrine,
        my madness will be gone . . . like that!
And I will speed you home again, to Mykene,
        in our swift-oared ship.
Dear sister, beloved sister, save me.
Save the house of our fathers.
I am lost and the line of Pelops blotted out,
        unless we get that little goddess
        dropped from heaven.

Choral Leader

Some strange demonic wrath
        storms against the seed of Tantalos
        and drives them through a gauntlet of pain.

143

Iphigenia

How I longed, Orestes, before you came,
    to stand again on Argive soil,
        and to look upon you, my long-lost brother.
My will is to echo yours, to lift from you your affliction
    and to heal a stricken house.
I will tame the wildness I reared within me
    toward a father who would murder me.
I will do my part to put his house in order.
And so I will be spared your polluting sacrifice
    and rescue my own family.

But how do I elude a watchful goddess?
And the king is not to be discounted.
I fear what he will do when he finds an empty pedestal.
How will I then sidestep death?
What could be my defense?
Yet the risk would be sweet and so well-taken,
    if only, in one availing act,
    you could sweep up me and the stolen image
        into your well-trimmed ship.

Either I escape or die, I know that much.
But I also know that, with or without me, you may succeed
    and win a safe journey home.
Not one inch will I shy back from saving you,
    even if I must pay for it with my life.
When a man dies, his house is forever empty.
But when a woman dies, she is forgotten.

Orestes

Already I have murdered my mother.
I am not about to murder you.
Mother's blood is enough to stain my hands.
From now on I want to live at one with you,
    or else die as one with you.
If there is a way out of here, a way home, I lead you down it.
If there is not, we shall both remain
    and face a common death.

144

Listen to what I am thinking.
Is it likely that Loxias would have bidden me
        to bring the holy image to the city of Athena,
        or even arranged for me to see your face again,
                if the whole scheme
        were sheer effrontery to Artemis?
No, I think there is a conspiring here in our favor,
        and so I am hopeful, Sister, for our homecoming.

Iphigenia

But how are we going to carry off the statue
        and both escape?
This is where our homecoming runs aground.
I think what we need is a plan.

Orestes

Couldn't we just kill the king?

Iphigenia

You propose something dreadful:
        for a guest to slay a host.

Orestes

Dreadful or not, it must be dared
        if you and I are going to escape.

Iphigenia

I admire your zeal, brother.
But that I couldn't do.

Orestes

What if you hid me away
        deep within the temple?

Iphigenia

So that we might escape later,
        cloaked in the darkness?

Orestes

Of course.
Daylight is fine, when you've nothing to hide.
But night suits thieves best.

Iphigenia

The temple has many guards.
We can't just walk past them.

Orestes

Then we're ruined.
I see no escape, do you?

Iphigenia

I think I have a new trick we haven't thought to try.

Orestes

What kind of trick? Tell me, so I may know.

Iphigenia

We shall turn your famed affliction to our own advantage . . .
with a little guile.

Orestes

Women hatch schemes like they do children,
with very little prompting.

Iphigenia

I will say you are a matricide from Argos.

Orestes

Use my wretchedness for what it is worth to us.

Iphigenia

I will say you are unfit for sacrifice.

146

Orestes

To what end? I think I may know.

Iphigenia

Unclean. You are unclean.
I give only pure victims up to slaughter.

Orestes

What does any of this have to do with stealing the statue?

Iphigenia

I will propose to cleanse you at sea,
⠀⠀⠀⠀with waters drawn from pure sea-springs.

Orestes

But I sailed here for the statue, and it's still in the temple.

Iphigenia

Then it too must be cleansed. I will say you touched it.

Orestes

Where will this take place?
In the breakers off the nearby cape?

Iphigenia

Where your ship lies moored, tied fast with lines of hemp.

Orestes

Will you or someone else carry the statue?

Iphigenia

I will. I alone may touch it sinlessly.

Orestes

What of Pylades? What part does he play in all of this?

Iphigenia

I will say his hands bear the same polluting stain as yours.

Orestes

And the king? Will he know what you plan to do,
        or will you keep it from him?

Iphigenia

I see no way to keep him in the dark.
I will sway him to the sense of what I do.

Orestes

Well, my ship lies ready,
        its oars poised to plow the seas.

Iphigenia

That part and whatever follows I leave to you.

Orestes

One more thing we will need,
        the silence of these girls who wait on you.
Find whatever words will win or beg them to our side.
Ply the special power you women have
        for wringing pity from a rock,
                much less from other women.
Then we'll hope the rest goes well for us.

Iphigenia

Turning to the Chorus.

Dearest women, I look at you and see
        that everything depends on you.
Whether I succeed or fail,
        whether I win or lose my dear homeland,
                all this is in your hands.
Let me begin my appeal to you here,
        on our most common ground.

We are all women.
The good will we bear each other
        runs as deeply in us as our blood.
We are the most watchful guardians of our common trust.
Keep silence and help secure our flight.
A well-kept tongue is cause for no slight praise.
You see the three of us, yoked in love
        and set upon a daring venture.
Either we shall reach the home of our fathers
        or we shall die in the attempt.

And if I escape,
        I will return and see to your escape as well.
My good fortune shall be a cup
        from which we all shall drink our fill.
Take my hand and swear . . . you . . . and you . . .

Iphigenia passes among the women, grasping their hands,
touching their faces and falling to her knees, a suppliant.

I beg you . . . by your dear cheek . . . by your knees . . .
        by all those you love and treasure at home.
What do you say?
Who is with me?
Who is unwilling?
Say something!
Without you, without some approving word from you,
        my hapless brother and I are as good as dead.

Choral Leader

Take cheer, dear lady, and see to your escape.
Our lips will say no more than stones would
        about your plans.
Great Zeus above will witness to this pledge of ours.

Iphigenia

May the gods reward you for these words . . .
        with great happiness.
Good-bye, my friends.

Iphigenia embraces the Chorus one at a time.

Turning to Orestes and Pylades.

The next step is yours.
Go inside the temple.
The king will be along any moment now.
He will want to know if the strangers' sacrifice
   has been accomplished.

Orestes and Pylades enter the temple, and Iphigenia lifts her hands in prayer.

O goddess,
   once atop the cliffs of Aulis you saved me
     from my father's dread murderous hand.
Save me again now . . . and those I love.
Otherwise you will carry the burden of blame,
   if never again men heed the words of Loxias.
Be gracious and abandon this barbarous land for Athens.
This country far from suits you,
   while in Athens a city blessed by gods awaits you.

Chorus

Halcyon,
Denizen of sea-carved cliffs,
Bird of a darkest song.
Keen hearts rend at your mourning
Laments for a mate long lost.
Without the grace of winged flight,
A grave heart within me
Echoes the saddest of your songs.
For the noisy fellowship of the market,
For blessed Artemis worshipped with joy
By the Kynthian hill,
I cry out with longing.
As a bird craves the open sky,
I crave the once familiar palm and laurel,
The sacred silvered olive boughs,
Kind to Leto in her labor,
The glistening pool slowly spun in circles
By a swan singing service
To the Muses.

When my city fell,
My tears ran like angry rivers
Until my face was rutted with my pain.
Dragged through the ruins of all I loved,
I was cast aboard the conqueror's ship,
A prize stowed among the oars and spears.
Sold for someone's price, they shipped me here
To do barbarous service in a barbarous land.
My office is to wait upon the child of Agamemnon
And hers to offer sacrifice not of sheep but men
To deer-slaying Artemis on an altar soaked with death.
How I envy those whose lives of pain are seamless,
Innocent of joy.
They have formed the habits that I need.
And their doom may lift like a passing storm.
But when ruin visits the unexpecting house,
Its companion is despair.

You, lady, are homeward bound,
Aboard a gallant Argive ship
Fitted with fifty oaken oars,
Tilling the untamed seas with rhythmic force,
Quickened and cadenced by the shrill piping
Of a reed and waxen flute,
Sweet to the ears of mountain-leaping Pan.
Phoibos, prolific in his prophecies,
Plucks his seven-stringed lyre and
Lifts a joyous song to hearten and direct
Your journey home to Argos' fertile plains.
Lifted through the churning sea
By straining arms on salt-soaked oars,
You will feel the spray across your face
And watch the raving winds blast the open sail.
But the prow that points and cuts your course
Turns from me
Forsaken.

How I would soar to the luminous course
Where the sun's flaming steeds
Lift the day from night.

I would not rest from winged flight
Until I hovered over the walls and the roofs
That once sheltered my youth.
There I would join the festive company,
As once, a blushing girl beside the splendid bride,
I danced amidst a whirling maze of friends,
And watched my mother smiling wistfully.
Wakened to the rivalry of youth and beauty,
I strew my charms for all to wonder at,
Resplendent robes and a child's soft hair
That blew across my face and glistened
Like a spray of gold.

Thoas enters, attended.

Thoas

Where is the keeper of the temple, the Greek woman?
Has she seen to the strangers' sacrifice?
Are they ablaze yet in the sanctuary?

Choral Leader

King, she is here to tell you clearly all that needs telling.

Iphigenia enters, carrying in her arms the image of Artemis.

Thoas

What is this? Child of Agamemnon,
        why do you carry in your arms the holy image?
Why have you removed it from its sacred pedestal?

152

Iphigenia

King, stay where you are in the portico.
Don't move.

Thoas

Iphigenia, what happened in there?

Iphigenia

Spitting, to avert an evil omen.

Silence!
This is prescribed.

Chanting.

O awesome spirit . . .

Thoas

Wait!
Why this strange invocation?
Explain yourself.

Iphigenia

Defilement, King.
Unclean. Unclean.
The victims you snared for me are unfit.

Thoas

Is this some feeling that you have?
Or do you have some proof?

Iphigenia

On her holy pedestal
      the goddess turned and faced the other way.

Thoas

On her own?
Or did the earth quake and rattle her around?

153

Iphigenia

On her own.
She also shut her eyes.

Thoas

And the reason, you say,
        is some pollution from the strangers?

Iphigenia

Yes, nothing else.
They are guilty of a heinous crime.

Thoas

Did they murder one of my people on the beach?

Iphigenia

They came with murder on their hands,
        murder in their own home.

Thoas

Now you've given me an appetite
        to know these things.
Tell me. Who was their victim?

Iphigenia

It was their mother they cut down.
Like two woodsmen,
        they shared the bloody labor.

Thoas

Apollo!
No barbarian would be as bold as that.

Iphigenia

They've been hounded out
        of every city and cave in Hellas.

154

Thoas

Then they are the reason
　　why you carry the goddess outside here?

Iphigenia

Yes, into the pure and hallowed air, for its chastening.

Thoas

How did you learn the source of their defilement?

Iphigenia

When the goddess turned her back on them,
　　I began to ask them questions.

Thoas

Well done.
They make smart girls in Greece.

Iphigenia

Clever boys as well.
These Greeks have already cast sweet bait before me
　　in hopes of hooking my heart.

Thoas

What do they use to lure you with?
Bits of news from Argos?

Iphigenia

They say my only brother, Orestes, is alive and well.

Thoas

Hoping you will spare them out of gladness at their news?

Iphigenia

They say my father lives and prospers.

155

Thoas

Of course you turned your back on them,
        in allegiance to the goddess.

Iphigenia

Of course I did. Greece ruined me and I hate her for it.

Thoas

Then tell me, what do we do with these strangers?

Iphigenia

We must do what is prescribed by sacred ordinance.

Thoas

Then we just put to use your lustral waters and your knife,
        don't we?

Iphigenia

No, we don't.
I must purify them first with cleansing ablutions.

Thoas

Does that mean spring water or salt water?

Iphigenia

It is the sea that washes off the sins of men.

Thoas

All the more suitable they will be for slaughter.

Iphigenia

And all the more suitable for my purposes.

Thoas

Well, the waves wash up very near the shrine, yes?

Iphigenia

Yes. But we require seclusion;
    for there is more that needs to be done.

Thoas

You see to it.
I am not one to pry into matters not intended for my eyes.

Iphigenia

The goddess must, too, be cleansed.

Thoas

If the mother-slayers sullied her.

Iphigenia

If they had not, I never
    would have moved the goddess from her pedestal.

Thoas

I commend your piety and your care.

Iphigenia

There are things I need done.

Thoas

You need only tell me what they are.

Iphigenia

The strangers must be bound.

Thoas

Where could they flee?

Iphigenia

No matter. They are Greeks, and Greeks cannot be trusted.

Thoas

To his Attendants.

Men, go and bind the strangers.

Iphigenia

And I want them brought here.

Thoas

As you say.

Iphigenia

With their heads covered.

Thoas

I see . . . in case they might pollute the light of day.

Several Attendants go off into the temple.

Iphigenia

I will need some of your henchmen with me.

Thoas

Indicating several of his Attendants.

These will go with you.

Iphigenia

And you must send word throughout the city . . .

Thoas

Word of what?

Iphigenia

That everyone must stay indoors.

Thoas

Lest anyone meet eyes with the murderers . . .

Iphigenia

And contract their dread stain.

Thoas

Dispatching one of his Attendants.
Go and do as the priestess has said.

Iphigenia

I am most concerned for those I love.

Thoas

Including me.

Iphigenia

No one must be near enough to see them.

Thoas

You overlook nothing in your care for me and my city.

Iphigenia

I hope you are right.

Thoas

I know I am right in saying
        that the whole city wonders at you.

Iphigenia

King, it is for you to remain here before her shrine.

Thoas

Doing what?

159

Iphigenia

Cleansing it with fire.

Thoas

For your return, so that you may find it pure.

Iphigenia

But before that . . .
   when the strangers come out here . . .

Thoas

What do I do then?

Iphigenia

Pull your cloak over your eyes.

Thoas

Against their contagion?

Iphigenia

And if I seem to be away too long . . .

Thoas

How long would be too long?

Iphigenia

Let's not wonder about that.

Thoas

All in good time, you will do your sacred duty.

Iphigenia

Let us pray for this ritual,
   that it may go as planned.

Thoas

Let us pray.

The temple doors open. Several Guards and Attendants lead out Orestes and Pylades, whose hands are bound and heads covered. Thoas throws his cloak over his head as instructed.

Iphigenia

See, the strangers come from the shrine.
With them are carried my sacred robes
        and the two newborn lambs.
Blood for blood, untainted for tainted,
        the one will wash away the other's stain.

To the Attendants.

Good, you have brought the burning lamps
        and all else I ordered
      for the cleansing of the strangers and the goddess.

Iphigenia raises high the image of the goddess and the procession forms behind her.

All people of this city, hear me.
Stand back and avoid defilement.
All ye servants of the sanctuary,
      whose hands are pure for the service of Artemis;
All ye espoused ones, come to make your wedding vows;
All ye mothers heavy with child,
Away!
Flee, lest the pollution spread to you.

O mistress, virgin daughter of Zeus and Leto,
      if I cleanse these victims of all stain
        and make of them a fitting sacrifice,
    once more your home shall be free of taint
        and we shall be glad.
Of the rest I say nothing.
In silence I commend my heart's desire
        to you, goddess and your fellow-gods,
     who read our hearts and know all we fail to say.

Chorus

On Delos once,
Sheltered by gracious boughs bright with fruit,
Leto bore a splendid son, a god with golden hair,
Whose fingers make the lyre sing;
A daughter too, goddess of the bow and quiver,
Whose arrows find their mark.
Then Leto left the site of their famed birth,
And from a ridge girt by glistening sea
Brought her son to towering Parnassos,
Mount of thunderous torrents,
Mount of bakkhant revels.
There the giant serpent,
Livid-eyed and scaly-backed,
Lay coiled among the shading laurel.
Dread and massive beyond report,
The monstrous Python kept grim guard
Over the ancient chthonic oracle.

But you, Phoibos, still a tiny babe,
A lively armful for your dearest mother,
You, Phoibos, slew the great serpent
And seized the sacred oracle.
Seated now upon your golden tripod,
Your throne immune from error,
Beside the pure Kastalian springs,
You make your home at the center of the world,
And from your secret sanctuary,
You send upon us mortals
The sweet dew of your divine decrees.

162

Now when Apollo drove out Themis, daughter of Earth,
From the seat of holy oracles,
Then Earth spawned dreams instead.
These fluctuating phantoms, born in dead of night,
Visit cities as they sleep
And fashion vague accounts of what once was
And of what is yet to be.
This was Earth's revenge,
For what her sister suffered.
Soon enough her dreams would steal
Apollo's pride and place.
But lord Apollo fell into a fitful rage at this,
And up the steep Olympian slopes
Ran with winged feet
To the very throne of Zeus,
And clung there with an infant's needy grip,
Pleading for an end to Earth's avenging dreams.
Then Zeus smiled on his beloved son,
Amused at his frenzy and his haste
In claiming the golden spoils of piety.
Zeus nodded his assent,
And silenced night's revealing voices.
He banished any truth from visions dreamed in sleep,
And restored to his son every honor lost.
Zeus gave his word to ground the trust
Borne by all who throng the seat of truth
For words of purest light.

The Messenger enters.

Messenger

Guards . . . attendants!
Where is King Thoas? Where can I find the king?
Throw open the temple doors and summon out here
      the ruler of this land.

Choral Leader

What's wrong?
If you can tell us, what is it?

Messenger

Gone! The two strangers are gone.
The child of Agamemnon schemed their escape.
They've run off and taken the holy goddess with them.
Stashed her in the hold of their ship,
        bound for Greece.

Choral Leader

I don't believe my ears!
But you want to see the king. He isn't here.
He left the temple in a hurry, not long ago.

Messenger

He must be told what's happened. Where did he go?

Choral Leader

How would we know?
Now run off and look for him.
And when you find him, tell him your news.

Messenger

Wait.
Where there is one contriving woman,
        there may be many more.
You women breed among yourselves.
All of you have had a share in this.

Chorus

Have you lost your wits?
What does the strangers' escape have to do with us?
Now, get lost.
You would do well to run your fastest to the palace gates.

Messenger

Not so fast. I'm not leaving until I get an answer
        to my question . . . from behind those doors.
Is the king in there or not?

Unbolt the doors!

Pounding on the doors.

Open up in there!
Tell your king that someone waits out here for him
        with the worst of news.

The temple doors swing open and Thoas enters.

Thoas

Who are you, making such an uproar
        on the goddess' very threshold?
Why were you pounding at the doors
        and throwing your noisy voice inside?

Messenger

These women lied to me.
They told me you had left,
        even though you were still inside.
They were trying to get rid of me.

Thoas

But why?
What would they hope to gain from doing that?

Messenger

I will get to them later.
But listen now to what is more urgent.
The girl . . . the one who served here at the altar . . .
        Iphigenia.
She's run away with the strangers.
And they've taken the holy image of the goddess.
That cleansing business was a trick.

Thoas

What are you saying?
What possessed her to do that?
I don't understand.

165

Messenger

Well, this will make it worse;
      but she did it to save Orestes.

Thoas

Orestes, the son of Klytemnestra?

Messenger

He was the one prepared for sacrifice.

Thoas

A miracle. I know no other name for it.

Messenger

Never mind its name.
Listen to me.
Once you've heard and pondered all I have to tell,
      we'll need a plan from you,
          some strategy for our pursuit of them.

Thoas

You're making sense. Go on.
If they are hoping to outrun my spear,
      they have a long road ahead of them.

Messenger

As soon as we had come to the shore,
      near where Orestes' ship lay in secret mooring,
    the child of Agamemnon shouted to us,
      the men you sent along to guard the strangers.
    and waved us back with her arms.
"Back . . . stand back," she ordered us, "all of you stand off."
Then she lit the sacrificial flame and began the cleansing rites
    for which we'd come.
She took in her hands the rope that held the two men bound
    and walked off with them alone,
      they in front and she behind them.

166

I for one began to grow suspicious, king,
        but your servants found everything in order.
Time was passing and the priestess saw the need to assure us
        that something was, in fact, taking place.
So she let out a piercing cry and began to chant
        some wild mystical mutterings,
                suited, we supposed, for washing blood.
But then a long time passed . . . too long.
We waited and we thought at last
        that the strangers may have gotten loose,
        killed the priestess, fled, and sailed away.
But still we sat in silence,
        fearing to see what was forbidden to our eyes.

At last we set aside all that we'd been told
        and agreed to go and find them.
Soon we spied a Greek galley, fitted out with fifty oars,
        like a hawk with fifty wings,
           each oar held poised above the pitching sea
                by a Greek seaman ready at his bench.
Then we saw the two strangers,
        standing free near the galley's stern.
With long poles several seamen steadied the ship's prow,
        while others hoisted anchor, pulled up cables,
        and dropped a ladder for the strangers
           into the churning sea.
We were undaunted when we saw their wiles at work.
We fell on them at once and seized the girl.
We grabbed the mooring cables.
We reached through the stern ports
        and tried to drag out the rudder-oars.
We mixed shouts with our struggles:
 "Tell us what right you think you have
        to steal from this land,
        running off with our priestess and our sacred image?
Who do you think you are to kidnap this girl?"
This was his reply:
"I am that girl's brother.
I am Orestes, son of Agamemnon.
I am taking home the sister that I lost."

167

But his words weakened not at all the grip we had on the girl,
    nor our resolve to drag her back to you.
You see from my face the battering that we took
    to do just that.
Neither they nor we had weapons at our sides;
    and so it was a battle of fists and feet.
The two strangers flew at us with such frenzied force,
    pounding and kicking us front and back
        no matter where we turned,
    that it was as brief as it was brutal
        before our legs gave way.
Bruised and bloodied, we made a sorry sight
    as we scrambled up the nearest crag,
        with heads aching and eyes swelling closed.
Yet once we reached a vantage point
    above them on the rocks,
    we took up the war again
        and sent down a hail of stones on them.
But soon they put an end to this, with a line of archers
    standing on the galley's stern.
Their whizzing arrows soon sent us on our way.

Just then a crashing wave broke against the Greek ship's hull
    and lifted it towards shore.
Iphigenia shuddered at the swirling foam
    as Orestes lifted her from the threatening sea
        and placed her on his left shoulder.
Then he strode through the surf,
        mounted the swaying sea-ladder,
    and set down on the ship's deck his sister and
        the heaven-fallen image of the child of Zeus.
From mid-ships came a sudden cry:
"Greeks, seamen, grip your oars and plow white the sea.
We have what we came for.
We have done what we crossed the hostile sea
    and risked the clashing rocks to do."
From the belly of the ship thundered their response,
    one rending shout of triumph,
    as they shouldered their oars
        against the unwelcoming sea.

168

While still within the bay, their way was easy,
      and they skimmed over the gentle breakers.
But when they cleared the bay's mouth and struck
      the untamed sea, the struggle began.
A wild blast of wind spun the ship around
      and hurled it back against its course.
But the Greeks met the challenge
      and fought the sea straight on.
All the same the ship was being driven back to land
      by a contrary sea.
Then the daughter of Agamemnon rose
      and stood upon the deck.
She lifted her arms in prayer:
"O child of Leto, I am your priestess. Save me.
From this land of barbarians bring me home to Greece.
Forgive my theft.
Goddess, you know how you love your brother.
See how I too love my brother and my family."
In concert with the girl's prayers,
      the seamen hymned their own plea,
         while their bare shoulders flexed
         and their ready hands plied the oars,
      keeping the coxswain's time.

Each moment now brought them closer to the rocks.
One of us splashed into the sea and waded towards the ship
      while others made nooses out of rope
         to snare the ship and drag it to the rocks.
I, for my part, came back here at once to you, my king,
      to let you know what's happening there.

Now come at once. Bring ropes and nooses!
For unless the sea calms,
      the strangers' hope of deliverance is a stale dream.
Dread Poseidon, lord of seas, is still watchful over Troy
      and set against the house of Pelops.
And now he prepares to hand over to you and to your people
      the son of Agamemnon, and the daughter,
         who forgot the death she nearly died on Aulis
         and betrayed the one who saved her.

169

Choral Leader

Ill-starred Iphigenia, you and our brother
       will soon slip back in our master's hands,
          this time to die.

Thoas

Listen to me . . . everyone!
I want every man in this barbarian land
       to bridle and mount his horse.
Now! Gallop to the shore
       and intercept the Greek ship as it runs aground.
Let the goddess lead you in the hunt
       as you ferret out your wretched prey.
Now, sailors,
       drag your swift-oared ships down into the waves.
We shall run them down by land and sea,
       and fling their bodies from the cliffs
          or spit them on our spears alive.
As for you women who had your share in all of this,
          your punishment will have to wait
       until I have a moment free.
For now my hands are full,
       and I haven't time to waste on you.

Athena

Appearing overhead.

King Thoas, just where do you think you're off to?
What sort of hunt is this?
Listen to what I, Athena, tell you.
Cease this mad pursuit of yours.
Call in your troops.
It was decreed by Loxias himself
       that Orestes should come here
          to escape the furies' rage
       and to take his sister home to Argos.
When he removes the sacred image to my land
          and wins release from his present agony,
       he does Apollo's bidding.

This is what I say to you:
This design you have --
      to seize Orestes in the surf
           and relieve him of his life --
      it shall not be.
For even now on my behalf,
          Poseidon lulls the sea to sleep
      to make light work for Greek oars.

And now, Orestes, consider my command to you.
For even from afar you hear the voice of Artemis.
Go now, with your sister and the graven image.
Go to Athens, the city crafted by the gods.
From there seek out a sacred place, a place we call Halas,
      on the Attic border, near the Karustian hills.
There construct a temple to house the holy image
        and bestow on it a name reminiscent of this place
           and of the agony that was yours
        as you moaned your way through Greece,
        a wretched vagrant stunned by the furies' rage.
In time to come that temple will resound
      with hymns to Taurian Artemis.
And this will be the law you will establish there,
        at the yearly festival:
      in completion of the sacrifice left unfinished here,
      the priest shall press his blade
          against a young man's neck,
        until his bright blood flows
      in ritual praise of Artemis and to keep intact her pride.

You, Iphigenia, shall preside over the temple of the goddess
        on the terraces of Brauron,
      and keep her holy keys again.
There you shall die and be laid to rest.
And as tokens on your honor,
        women shall drape your tomb with lovely gowns,
          woven of the finest threads,
        and left behind by women in their beds,
          who gave their lives in giving life,
      exhausted in their labor.

Now you, Thoas, I charge
    to send these Greek women home,
        where their righteous hearts deserve to be.

Orestes, already I saved you once on the Areopagos,
    tipping the balanced scales to your side.
And what I did then shall now be law.
When the jury's votes are tied,
        the verdict shall be innocence,
    as it was for you.
Now, I saved you a second time.
Go, son of Agamemnon,
    take your sister out of this land.

One last time I tell you, Thoas,
    put out your rage now,
        as you would an unwelcome fire.

Thoas

Lady Athena,
    anyone who hears the words from the gods above
        and heedless goes his own way,
    lets his mind run loose like a wild horse.
I bear no malice towards Orestes and his sister.
Let them take the holy image and go.
My fire is out.
What sort of prize could I win,
    wrestling with the gods who have all the power?
Let the two of them take the graven goddess
    to your land and to the pedestal prepared for it.
In all of this, they have my blessing.

As for these Greek women,
    I send them home to happiness.
That was what you said. That is what I do.
There shall be no attack on the strangers.
I shall stay every spear
    and see our ships dragged back on land.
All this in keeping with your will, goddess.

Athena

Well done, Thoas. You are no fool.
You, no less, than the god themselves,
      must bend to fate or break.
Winds, rise from sleep,
          fill the sails of the son of Agamemnon,
     and lift him to Athens in the palm of your hand.
In this journey -- to watch over the image of my sister --
     I too will companion him.

Chorus

Go your way with all good fortune.
You are blessed to have your fates reversed,
      and to win deliverance from exile and from death.
O splendid goddess, Pallas Athena,
         wonder to men and gods alike,
    what you say is what we do.
Our hearts aspire to no joy nor hope
     beyond the words you give us.

SUGGESTED READINGS

Greek Mythology and Religion

Burkert, Walter, *Structure and History in Greek Mythology and Ritual* (Berkeley: University of California, 1979)

Burkert, Walter, *Homo Necans: The Anthropology of Ancient Greek Sacrificial Ritual and Myth* (Berkeley, University of California, 1983)

Burkert, Walter, *Greek Religion* (Cambridge: Harvard University, 1985)

Detienne, Marcel, *The Creation of Mythology* (Chicago: University of Chicago, 1986)

Loraux, Nicole, *Tragic Ways of Killing a Woman* (Cambridge: Harvard University, 1987)

Vernant, Jean-Pierre, *The Origins of Greek Thought* (Ithaca: Cornell University, 1982)

Vernant, Jean-Pierre, *Myth and Society in Ancient Greece* (New York: Zone, 1988)

Vernant, Jean-Pierre and Vidal-Naquet, Pierre, *Myth and Tragedy in Ancient Greece* (New York: Zone, 1988)

Vernant, Jean-Pierre, *Mortals and Immortals* (Princeton: Princeton University, 1991)

Veyne, Paul, *Did the Greeks Believe in Their Myths?* (Chicago: University of Chicago, 1988)

Vidal-Naquet, Pierre, *The Black Hunter: Forms of Thought and Forms of Society in the Greek World* (Baltimore: Johns Hopkins, 1986)

175

Greek Theatre

Herington, John, *Poetry Into Drama: Early Tragedy and the Greek Poetic Tradition* (Berkeley: University of California, 1985)

Ley, Graham, *A Short Introduction to the Ancient Greek Theatre* (Chicago: University of Chicago, 1991)

Simon, Erika, *The Ancient Theatre* (London: Methuen, 1982)

Stanford, W.B., *Greek Tragedy and the Emotions* (London: Routledge & Kegan Paul, 1983)

Taplin, Oliver, *Greek Tragedy in Action* (Berkeley: University of California, 1978)

Euripides

Arrowsmith, William, "A Greek Theatre of Ideas" *Arion* II:3, Autumn 1963, pp. 32-56.

Dodds, E.R., *The Greeks and the Irrational* (Berkeley: University of California, 1951)

Foley, Helene P., *Ritual Irony: Poetry and Sacrifice in Euripides* (Ithaca: Cornell University, 1985)

Meagher, Robert, *Mortal Vision: The Wisdom of Euripides* (New York: St. Martin's, 1989)

Powell, Anton, ed., *Euripides, Women, and Sexuality* (New York: Routledge, Chapman and Hall, 1990)

Vellacott, Philip, *Ironic Drama* (London: Cambridge University, 1975)

Whitman, Cedric, *Euripides and the Full Circle of Myth* (Cambridge: Harvard University, 1974)